D0776549

everything is sacred
An Introduction to the Sacrament of Baptism
Thomas J. Scirghi, SJ

Foreword by James Martin, SJ

PARACLETE PRESS
BREWSTER, MASSACHUSETTS

Everything Is Sacred: An Introduction to the Sacrament of Baptism

2012 First Printing

Copyright © 2012 by Thomas J. Scirghi

ISBN 978-1-55725-676-8

Scripture quotations marked RSV are taken from the *Revised Standard Version of the Bible*, copyright © 1946, 1952, 1971 by the Division of Christian Education of the National Council of the Churches of Christ in the USA. Used by permission.

Scripture quotations marked ESV are taken from *The Holy Bible, English Standard Version® (ESV®)*. Copyright ©2001 by Crossway Bibles, a division of Good News Publishers. Used by permission. All rights reserved.

Scripture quotations marked NAB are taken from the *New American Bible with Revised New Testament and Revised Psalms* © 1991, 1986, 1970 Confraternity of Christian Doctrine, Washington, D.C., and are used by permission of the copyright owner. All Rights Reserved. No part of the *New American Bible* may be reproduced in any form without permission in writing from the copyright owner.

Library of Congress Cataloging-in-Publication Data

Scirghi, Thomas J.
  Everything is sacred : an introduction to the sacrament of baptism / Thomas J. Scirghi ; foreword by James Martin.
    p. cm.
  ISBN 978-1-55725-676-8 (trade pbk.)
  1. Baptism. I. Title.
  BV811.3.S35 2012
  234'.161--dc23   2011053410

10 9 8 7 6 5 4 3 2 1

Published by Paraclete Press
Brewster, Massachusetts
www.paracletepress.com
Printed in the United States of America

contents

foreword

A few years ago, I attended the First Holy Communion of the daughter of one of my cousins. As a priest, I had been invited to concelebrate the Mass with the local bishop, who proved himself to be a friendly, garrulous man.

The church was packed with beaming parents and nervous children, proud but uncomfortable in their new suits and white dresses. As often happens during many of these Masses, the bishop began by asking the boys and girls some easy questions, as a way not only of testing their knowledge about what (and Who) they were about to receive, but of drawing them into the ceremony.

"What is the first sacrament of initiation?" he said to the children seated in the first few rows.

"Baptism," they all shouted.

"Very good," said the bishop, and I saw the director of religious education relax visibly.

"Now boys and girls, during what sacrament do we first receive the Holy Spirit?"

"Baptism!" they shouted even more loudly. Then, in an unscripted aside, he turned to me and said, in a barely audible whisper, "The answer to almost *any* question about the sacraments is baptism."

Baptism is the answer. The first of the traditional seven sacraments. The "gateway," to use a beautiful spiritual image, to the rest of the sacraments. The first time that a Christian "receives," in any sort of formalized way, the gift of the Holy Spirit. The first, as those children knew, of the great sacraments of "initiation." The beginning of a person's life in the community of the church. Baptism has been the "answer" for a very long time. It marked, in a dramatic way, the initiation of Jesus (by John the Baptist) into his public ministry, and was the time when, according to the Gospels, a heavenly sign proclaimed Jesus as the Son of God. For all those who doubted Jesus's place in salvation history, his baptism was part of the answer. But the baptism of Jesus was a sign not only of Jesus's divinity, but his humanity. The carpenter from Nazareth took his place, along with all the other believers, at the Jordan River to have John the Baptist pour water over his head. God stood in line at his baptism.

Baptism has also been the way that Christians, from the earliest days, welcomed new members into their community. Over the centuries, people have quite literally died for it: baptism into the Christian faith marked not only your inclusion in the community but your willingness to undergo persecution and even death.

The sacrament is also, arguably, the most beloved of the seven, at least among Catholics. Who doesn't enjoy a baptism? It is the most purely celebratory of sacraments. The parents are beaming; the grandparents are amazed that their own children now have children; the godparents are touched that they have been chosen for their roles. Unlike a wedding, for example, there is far less stress and angst. (Does anyone work themselves into frenzy about the "dress" that the baby is wearing?) Unlike a funeral, no one is paralyzed with grief. (On the other hand, the parents of a new child may be paralyzed with fatigue.) Unlike First Communion, there are no crabby participants. (If you've not been to a First Communion recently, you might be surprised at the number of sullen faces among the children.) Unlike Confirmation, there's no doubt about what's going on. ("Wait a minute. Didn't they already receive the Holy Spirit at baptism?") And unlike Holy Orders there is no confusion about the rite itself. ("What's going on *now*?" is a frequent question at an ordination.)

Baptism is, in a word, fun. The old joke among priests that they'd rather do ten baptisms than one wedding gets to the heart of this. With a minimum of fuss and a maximum of gratitude, it is the sacrament of joy.

And ever since the RCIA (Rite of Christian Initiation for Adults) programs, based on the reforms of the Second Vatican

Council, have encouraged parishes to see the Easter Vigil Mass as the proper time for adult baptisms, many more Catholics are witnessing the sacrament in a clearer light. It is not simply as a child's welcome, but also one of an adult choice.

But, surprisingly, the sacrament is still something of a "mystery" to many Catholics. And I don't mean a good mystery. Most Catholics understand its purpose, more or less. But too many Catholics are seeking answers to a great many questions surrounding this great sacrament. Here are the most common questions I've heard over the years: Isn't it better to get baptized when you're older, and can understand what you're doing? Does my baby have to be baptized immediately? Will my child go to hell, limbo, or purgatory if—God forbid—he or she dies before baptism? So should I do the baptism myself over the sink? Why are so many baptisms done during the Mass these days? Why do we use that oil anyway—isn't water enough? What's the role of the godparents? Do they have to be Catholics? Christians? Believers? These are questions from good Catholics that deserve good answers. For if people remain confused about baptism, they will be confused about the sacramental life of the church, and, by extension, their faith.

That's why this new book by Thomas J. Scirghi, SJ, is so very welcome. Frankly, this is the best book on baptism I've ever read. It's wise without being overly academic; inviting without being overly informal; and concise without being slapdash. Fr. Scirghi, a distinguished scholar, compassionate pastor, and popular teacher at Fordham University, is the perfect guide to the history, theology, and application of the sacrament.

Father Scirghi's book could easily become a standard introduction to the sacrament, and is the perfect guidebook for curious parents, enthusiastic newcomers, and confused cradle Catholics. After reading it, you'll understand why we invite parents to have their children baptized, and also why we baptize adults at the Easter Vigil Mass. You'll know the significance of the oil (and the candle) in the rite. And the next time you see a priest or deacon pour water over a child's head and pronounce the ancient baptismal formula, you'll have a richer appreciation for his words and his actions. This new book is, in a sense, the answer to the questions about the answer.

—James Martin, sj, is a Jesuit priest and author of several books, including *My Life with the Saints, The Jesuit Guide to (Almost) Everything,* and *Between Heaven and Mirth.*

This book about baptism began neither in church nor in a class, but in the family room, sitting with parents and godparents, preparing for the baptism of their children. Over the years, I have enjoyed many of these visits. I meet with these parents and godparents to discuss what we will do in the upcoming ceremony—and why. For many family members, it is a refresher course in the Catholic tradition, but for just as many, it is new material. While many of the people involved show great interest for what we will soon celebrate, many of these same people also do not understand either the church's rituals or the faith that they profess. Cardinal Donald Wuerl, who heads the Committee on Doctrine for the United States Catholic Bishops, explained the problem recently by citing the "catechetical deficiencies" of the past decade. In his words, "The result is a generation or more of Catholics, including young adults today, who have little solid intellectual formation in their faith."[1]

With this problem in mind, I have attempted to explain the fundamental teaching of the Roman Catholic Church concerning the sacrament of baptism. Another way to describe my purpose would be to say that I hope to tell the story of Christianity from the perspective of the sacrament of baptism. Each of the seven sacraments tells the story of the Incarnation of God in Jesus Christ and how the presence of Christ is embodied in the church today. Sacraments likewise tell the story of Christians in their relationship with the Son of God and how we find the Holy Spirit at work in the world.

While all Christians celebrate sacraments in one form or another, I have written this book from within the Roman Catholic tradition. As a priest and a professor of sacramental theology, I have the great opportunity both to celebrate with members of the church as well as to analyze and reflect on these celebrations with my students. Since my ordination in 1986, I have had the privilege of baptizing many people, young and old, and aiding in their introduction to the Christian faith. Since 1996, I have had the opportunity to teach at one of the great Catholic institutions of higher education, Fordham University in New York City. Also, in 2001, I was invited to teach at the Jesuit School of Theology at Berkeley (now the Jesuit School of Theology at the University of Santa Clara in Berkeley). There I helped to prepare Jesuit seminarians for priesthood along with lay women and men for ecclesial lay ministry. The work on both coasts has provided me a rich experience in both theory and practice. As I have made my way along this academic route, I have discovered a large group of Roman Catholics who are devout in their practice of faith and well educated in the arts, sciences, or business but who have formally studied little theology. Still, their curiosity for the faith abounds. This book is intended for them. Nevertheless, while I write from a Roman Catholic perspective, I also hope that all Christians will find this book useful. We all might do well to focus on the meaning of baptism today, as well as on our common baptism, as we make our way toward church unity.

Now, a word about how we will proceed. As I intend to present the Christian story through the sacrament of baptism, I will begin by discussing sacraments in general. This is the subject of chapter 1: a brief review of sacramental theology with a focus on the "sacramental principle." In chapter 2, I then look at the sacrament of baptism itself. Here we will discuss the theological meaning of the absolution from sin and the incorporation into the body of Christ. We will also review the historical development of this sacrament. In chapter 3, I will explore the current ritual of baptism, with a focus on infant baptism. Finally, in chapter 4, I discuss several current "hot-button" issues concerning baptism, such as the state of limbo, the controversy over invoking the Trinitarian name, the proper minister of the sacrament, and a movement in which people wish to be "de-baptized," that is, to renounce their Christian heritage.

Saint Anselm, a Benedictine monk and theologian of the early twelfth century, explained the purpose of theology with the now-famous phrase *fides quaerens intellectum*, "faith seeking understanding." In other words, theology stands on a foundation of faith and reaches outward for greater understanding, which helps faith to grow. Without it, we are stagnant. Saint Augustine wrote something similar when he cried out in his *Confessions*: "Let me seek Thee, Lord . . . and let me utter my prayer believing in Thee. . . . My faith, Lord, cries to Thee, the faith that Thou hast given me."[2] I hope that this study of baptism may shed light on your understanding of your own Christian faith, and help to increase and deepen it all the while.

everything is sacred

The title of this book is not meant as a sentimental slogan, offering an overly optimistic view of the world, as if Christians were called to simply look on the bright side of life. Rather, Christians are challenged to see the hand of God in all of creation and to view our lives and our places in the world from this perspective.

This perspective reflects the meaning of the term *sacramental principle*, an important, recently rediscovered Catholic teaching according to which all of creation manifests the presence of God. The sea and sky, hills and valleys, flowers and fish, animals and humans, all reflect the Creator's hand. And by making good use of the gift of creation, we may realize the presence of the living God among us. Because we believe that the universe was created by God, we can learn something about the Creator through the creation.

For this reason, we can say that everything is sacred. The word *sacred* denotes something God considered especially dear and deserving of respect, as with something holy. All that comes from God is a gift; it is good. The proper use of creation expresses gratitude for the gift. By recognizing that all of creation is a gift of the Creator, we acknowledge that everything is sacred.

Saint John the Evangelist begins his Gospel on this note.

In the beginning was the Word, and the Word was with God, and the Word was God. He was in the beginning with God. All things came to be through him, and without him nothing came to be. What came to be through him was life, and this life was the light of the human race; the light shines in darkness, and the darkness has not overcome it. (Jn. 1:1–5 NAB)

The Word of God, that is, Jesus Christ, comes to shine light onto a blessed world, God's own creation. The presence of God shines through all of creation, especially through human beings, who are made in the image and likeness of God. But the world has grown dark from sin, as humans became distracted, hoarding the gift of creation and ignoring the giver.

You might recall the stories in the Gospels where Jesus restores sight to the blind. For example, you may recall the story of the blind man Bartimaeus (Mk. 10:46–52 RSV). He used to sit along the roadside that led to the city of Jericho, begging. One day, Jesus and his disciples, surrounded by a crowd, happen to be passing by. Bartimaeus senses the Lord's presence and shouts to him, "Son of David, have mercy on me!" Jesus halts in his tracks and his disciples bring the man to him. Bartimaeus stands before Jesus and pleads, "Master, let me receive my sight." Jesus responds, "Go your way; your faith has made you well." Immediately the man can see, and he follows Jesus. In a sense, Jesus' whole mission on earth could be thought of as just that—restoring sight to humanity.

However, the beginning of John's Gospel is not about a divine ability to restore physical sight. Rather, it is about *insight*, the cultivation of deeper understanding. When we gain insight, available from God alone, then the way in which we understand creation changes because, through the light of Christ, the world is given new meaning. We recognize this new meaning when we stand in a new relationship with God. The sacraments of the church provide a glimpse of spiritual insight, enabling us to recognize the presence of the Lord in our midst and to respond to his call.

Some everyday examples may help explain how this works. Say you pass a man on the way to work every day but barely notice him. Then one day, you meet him and discover that he is a friend of your good friend, and now this person stands out from the crowd of passersby. The person has not changed. What changed was the way in which you saw, or viewed, that man. In a similar way, I look at a coffee mug on my desk. It bears the seal of the United States Navy. It is an attractive cup and it is functional for a coffee break. But more than any other mug, this one holds special significance since a Navy chaplain gave it to me upon the completion of his degree program, for which I served as his director. This gift holds memory and meaning, not just coffee. A seemingly insignificant object or an action may take on new significance within the context of a relationship or through human experience.

Now, to be clear, I am not saying that the coffee mug itself is sacred. Rather, it points to something greater, namely, a memory of a human relationship. The significance of the object comes from what it points to beyond itself. That's also what sacraments do—but not with just any physical objects. Not with coffee mugs. Still, the principle holds true: small actions or ordinary physical things take on great significance for the same reason, in that they point beyond themselves.

Another example, this one within the setting of the church, is the custom of fasting for Lent. The purpose of the Lenten fast is to render us more dependent on God and less self-reliant. But think of the child desperately trying to abstain from chocolate throughout the forty days; it is a noble cause. However, often the child is challenged (so is an adult) when the focus of the fasting shifts away from one's relationship with God and toward the personal endurance of abstinence. Instead of having the goal of spiritual union with God, fasting becomes a temporal refraining from chocolate, a personal contest. For the action to have any lasting meaning, it must point beyond itself.

God the Artist

> God looked at everything he had made, and found it very good. (Gen. 1:31 NAB)

If we believe that God is truly the Creator of the universe—the Creator of all that exists—then we can know something of the creator though creation. We could say the same of any artist: we know something of the artist through his or her work. For example, we may marvel at Michelangelo as we look at the ceiling of the Sistine Chapel, or stare at the sculpture of his *Pietà* in St. Peter's Basilica. We may admire the genius that devised these works, his industry as we survey his numerous accomplishments, or his sensitivity to form as our eyes follow the fluid lines he etched in stone. Although we have never met the man, we know something about him through his creations. We glimpse the man through the material.

God is like an artist; all of created reality reveals the Creator. The poet Gerard Manley Hopkins, in his poem "God's Grandeur," imagines the world radiating the self-expressive beauty of the Creator.

The world is charged with the grandeur of God.

It will flame out like shining from shook foil.

It gathers to a greatness as the ooze of oil crushed.

Why do men then now not reck his rod.

Generations have trod, have trod, have trod.

And all is seared with trade. Bleared, smeared with toil.

And wear man's smudge, and share man's smell.

The soil is bare now, nor can foot feel being shod.

Yet for all this nature is never spent.

There lives the dearest, deepest fresh down things.

And though the last lights, off the black west went, oh
   morning,

at the brown brink eastward springs,

because the Holy Ghost over a bent world, broods with
   warm breast

and with Ah bright wings.[3]

Recognizing the Creator's hand in the work of creation is an essential part of understanding the sacramental principle: all created reality manifests the presence of God. Everything is sacred.

In the traditional teaching of the Catholic Church, we become aware of God's presence through visible and tangible things. We encounter God through people, places, and objects throughout the world. Moreover, it is only through created reality that we may encounter God.[4] Throughout the Old Testament, God reveals himself through the word spoken by the prophets. The Old Testament also describes the promise of the Lord with images that were attractive to Israel, for example, luscious banquets, a land flowing with milk and honey, or a fortress. In the Gospels, Jesus manifests the presence of God in tangible qualities, for example, through the physical healing of blindness or crippling disease; he feeds large crowds of people; he teaches in plain speech yet speaks with authority. It is through the material and within the context of faith that we encounter the spiritual.

The sacramental principle also points to another important teaching of the Catholic Church—the role of mediation between God and us. Every Catholic learns in catechism class that sacraments mediate the presence of God by revealing the supernatural through natural objects and practices. As a result, one is baptized with water and words, confirmed with oil, and fed the body and blood of Christ with bread and wine. These natural, everyday materials convey the presence of God to a community of believers. This is the purpose of the Christian sacraments: to mediate the presence of the divine in order to provide the faithful an encounter with God.

One never encounters God directly—only through a mediator. Likewise, we never really encounter another person fully. Our meeting with others is also and always mediated through language and customs that represent one person to another.

This notion of mediation sets Roman Catholics apart from many other Christian groups. Traditionally, Protestants are wary of ecclesiastical mediation between God and individuals, holding instead that an unmediated, person-to-person encounter with God is possible. Their objections are not without reason. Throughout the ages, sacramental worship has often been distorted, reducing a profound religious ritual into a magical and mechanical reality. Sacraments become magical when they are said to produce effects based solely on following the proper procedure: pronouncing the formula and performing the gestures. They become mechanical when it is thought that merely fulfilling the rubrics will restore a person to the state of grace. Following these lines of thought or practice, grace becomes a commodity rather than what it really is—a gift.

From the Latin *gratia*, grace means that which is pleasant, charming, or attractive. It also refers to "favor," either finding favor with others, or a favor done for another. Theologically speaking, grace is the favor of God's assistance so that human beings may respond to the divine call and participate in the life of God. It is a gratuitous gift from God. Through grace, God communicates himself to humanity, to which humans freely respond.[5] Saint Paul writes in his Letter to the Galatians, "[God] who had set me apart before I was born, and had called me through his grace, was pleased to reveal his Son to me, in order that I might preach him among the Gentiles" (Gal. 1:15–16 RSV).

You may remember learning about grace in grade school with a diagram of a milk bottle depicting a person's soul. I do. The analogy goes like this. When one is in the state of grace, the bottle is full of perfectly white, pure, cold, nutritious milk. But when one sins, the milk is depleted. And the more one sins, the less of the good stuff there is in the bottle. A trip to the confessional would offer a penitent spiritual refreshment and refill his or her "bottle." This magical or mechanical approach treats the sacraments as the means to manipulate God, as if by doing something for God we will get God to do something for us. In this analogy, it could appear as if we have been given the means to save ourselves. Coincidentally, the magic formula *hocus-pocus* possibly originated in the context of the celebration of the Eucharist during the Middle Ages. In the consecratory prayer over the bread, the priest would pronounce in Latin *hoc est enim corpus meum* ("This is my body"). Those unlearned in Latin may have heard it as *hocus-pocus*.

Some have compared this attitude to that of stopping at a gas station in which a person, finding her gas tank near empty, simply drives into a local station, pays her money, and pumps gas into the car, filling the tank and driving off. The mechanical approach treats the church like this—a "filling station" for grace. Missing here is any sense of growth in one's relationship with God. A healthy relationship in which two people are devoted to each other has no room for manipulation. The same holds true for one's relationship with the divine. Also missing from the magical or mechanical approach to sacramental worship is any sense of personal disposition. The faithful come to the altar with a conscious desire. We bring ourselves before the Lord, offering ourselves to God, standing ready to receive the Lord in word and sacrament.

This approach to the sacraments is the reason the Protestant Reformers grew suspicious of Catholic ritual. They sniffed out what was very clearly, often, sacramental superstition and thus contributed to a truer understanding of Christ's sacramental presence. Today the Catholic Church is careful to avoid any ✓ tendency toward superstition or divine manipulation.

Both Catholics and Protestants today need to consider the sacraments in light of the real presence of Jesus Christ. Paul Tillich, a Lutheran theologian, laments that, by removing or limiting sacramental celebration, Protestants may have lost the meaning of ritual. "Faith cannot remain alive without expressions of faith and the personal participation in them."[6] These expressions of faith and the personal participation in them must be mediated through language, symbols, and customs.

Indeed, we might ask if it could be possible to experience an immediate, or direct, encounter with the divine. What would such an encounter look or sound like? Even in revelation, God communicates in a manner that one can comprehend. So, while God may have spoken to Saint Francis of Assisi, commanding him to restore the church building of San Damiano, Francis would have heard the message in Italian, his own language. Likewise Saint Teresa of Avila saw a vision of herself with God, and this image was conveyed to her through bridal imagery, an image with which she was familiar. Even revelation must be mediated.

This does not limit God's power or freedom. While it is true that all things are possible for God (Matt. 19:26), the same cannot be said of human beings. Humans are limited and finite; we receive the Lord in a way appropriate for us. By way of analogy, imagine a teacher with a class of second-grade children. The teacher knows a great deal about a particular subject, while the children know very little. The teacher shows his creativity by conveying what he knows in a way that his students will comprehend. Good teachers, in other words, are recognized not simply for what they know but for how they mediate the material to their students. Jesus Christ, as our great teacher, mediates the presence of God to his students, his followers, in a way in which they may comprehend the message and draw closer to God.

The Mediating Power of Symbols

Sometimes we hear the comment, "that is just a symbol." Such a statement belies the power and efficacy of a symbol, suggesting that a symbol is the equivalent of a picture or a mere representative figure. But this does not capture what we mean at all. Sacraments are symbols, which means that, among other things, they are powerful devices of expression and communication.

Let's define our terms. The word *symbol* derives from the Greek word *symballein*, literally meaning "to throw together." In ancient times, a *symbolum* was used to establish a contract. When two parties entered into a contractual agreement, they would cut an object into two parts and each of the parties would retain one of the parts. For example, the parties might break a piece of pottery into two pieces, and each of the parties would hold one piece. When they or their representatives met again, they would present their individual pieces, and the broken, jagged edges would interlace, indicating that they were both part of the same vessel. The reunited object was the *symbolum*. Of course each only had value in its connection with the other half. Only in the act of meeting and "symbolizing" their two portions by joining them together did the two parties recognize the expression of the same contract. Moreover, the piece of pottery itself took on new meaning in this context. It was no longer a simple vessel, but a symbol of the act that joined the parties in a relationship. The agreement between the two partners established the symbol.

In defining "symbol" we need to distinguish it from a sign. Simply stated, a sign points to a reality but does not participate in it. But a symbol participates in the reality that is symbolized. For example, the highway destination sign seen on a Canadian highway, "USA—100 KM," is helpful in that it indicates the direction of the United States. However, this is very different from the sight of the American flag flying atop a flagpole. The connection between the highway sign and the country is purely functional, merely pointing the way. But the flag, as a symbol, evokes a sense of what it means to be American. And so we salute the flag and carry it in parades, and some of us get angry when it is desecrated. In contrast, hardly anyone except the staff of the highway department gets angry when a sign is damaged.

The celebration of the sacraments is a form of symbolic activity because the sacraments participate in the reality they symbolize. Sacraments do not merely point to the presence of God somewhere beyond us. They help us to encounter the presence of the living God. Jesus Christ is present to us in a unique way when we celebrate the sacraments.

Alongside the sacraments, we find "sacramentals," defined as sacred signs instituted by the church, which render the sacraments more fruitful and sanctify different aspects of daily life.[7] Besides the seven sacraments, the church provides specific rituals and objects that serve to unite the faithful in their quest for union with God. Sacramentals come in the form of objects such as the palm branches on Palm Sunday or a set of rosary beads. They also come in the form of ritual activity, such as praying a novena or receiving ashes on Ash Wednesday. All of these serve to mediate the presence of Christ and unite the Christian community in the practice of faith.

You have probably noticed that words always accompany sacraments. That is not by accident, and it is not because priests are overly talkative! Within Christian worship, stories serve to establish (or reestablish) the identity of the membership. We might think of such stories as symbolic speech, for these stories do not convey merely factual information, but evoke meaning and recognition. By juxtaposing an ancient story with a current situation, worshipers may understand themselves in a new way. In baptism, for example, a group of the faithful gathers to initiate a new member into the community. They listen to the Scripture, an ancient story of salvation as told by prophets and evangelists. Then the minister's preaching breaks open the Word of God and they hear how they play a part in the story. All of these words have power, and when they are combined with the power inherent in the sacraments themselves, we can honestly say that new life begins—both for the one being baptized and for the faithful who welcome him or her.

Word and sacrament—that is what our worship is all about. This is the reason for the two-part structure of the Mass: first the proclamation of the Word of God, followed by the reception of the sacrament. That the proclamation precedes the reception should ward off any notion of superstition as well as remind us that this celebration is not our own work. Rather, sacraments help to reveal the presence of God in our midst. Our worship does not conjure up the divine but opens our awareness of Christ's presence to be with us until the end of time.

The two-part structure is also intended to form a personal dynamic of "call and response," in which the Lord Jesus Christ calls to his people and they respond. The proclamation of the Scripture rehearses (i.e., repeats aloud) the story of salvation, recalling the elements of divine creation and redemption. It also articulates the call of Christ and the command to follow him. The people in turn demonstrate their desire to heed this call by approaching the Lord through the sacraments.

Efficacious, Instituted, and Entrusted

The Roman Catholic Church obviously thinks that sacraments are very important. They transform lives. They take human beings from birth to death, from present life to new life. But how exactly do they do this? The great theologians of the history of the church have occupied themselves with those very questions. According to the *Catechism of the Catholic Church*,

Sacraments are efficacious signs of grace, instituted by Christ and entrusted to the Church, by which divine life is dispensed to us. The visible rites by which the sacraments are celebrated signify and make present the graces proper to each sacrament. They bear fruit in those who receive them with the required dispositions. (no. 1131)

Let us look at this definition in some detail. First, sacraments are efficacious signs of grace. This means that they are not simply signs pointing to something beyond themselves; rather, they actually produce what they signify. They help Christians to express their faith. For example, the sacrament of baptism expresses the belief in the forgiveness of sin through rebirth in Jesus Christ. They also form Christians in the faith, which is to say that the celebration of the sacraments deepens the level of understanding of a person's faith as well as the commitment to serving God. Something happens during sacramental celebration as we hear the Word of God and respond to it wholeheartedly.

Consider a simple illustration. Imagine that you are looking at an elegantly dressed couple enjoying a romantic candlelight dinner in a fine French restaurant. They are celebrating their wedding anniversary. The setting itself could be construed as a sign of their affection for each other, a signal of romance. However, this dinner is more than a sign that merely points to something beyond itself. The event of a romantic ritual, eating a candlelit dinner at a French restaurant, should itself enhance the relationship of the couple. Their celebration marks the growth in their devotion for each other. Their being together in that setting and situation and with those specific markers of meaning does not just point to something external. All of that also produces an effect. Something actually happens.

Likewise, within sacramental celebration, something happens: we encounter the Lord. Sacramental celebrations are occasions through which God's presence is made available to

us in a unique way. The question is whether people realize this
and avail themselves of the grace. We will say more about this
a little later.

Second, sacraments are instituted by Christ. The word
instituted can be misleading if we think of it in terms of Jesus
of Nazareth establishing the rituals practiced within the
church today. Clearly Jesus did not baptize anyone, nor did he
officiate a wedding ceremony as far as we know. Nevertheless,
to say that the sacraments are instituted by Christ means that
they are founded on the teaching and action of Jesus during
his earthly ministry.

For example, we read in Scripture that he was baptized by
John in the Jordan River and that he shared a meal of bread
and wine with his disciples. In each case, Jesus commanded
his followers to continue these practices. For example, we hear
one command each time we gather for the Eucharist. At the
Last Supper, after distributing the bread and wine, and having
announced, "This is my body. . . . This is my blood" (Matt.
26:26–30 RSV), he commanded them, "Do this in remembrance
of me " (1 Cor. 11:24 RSV).[8]

Other sacraments, such as penance and anointing of the sick,
the two that specifically have to do with healing, are founded on
Jesus' care for the people he met and the numerous occasions
on which he forgave their sins and healed their wounds. Also,

when he sent his disciples out on mission in his name, he charged them to carry out these two tasks specifically.[9] Healing of both body and soul played an important part in Jesus' earthly ministry. The sacrament of holy orders—the commissioning of individuals for special service within the church—may be modeled on Jesus' call of the twelve apostles to carry on his work. The sacrament of marriage finds its roots in the covenantal relationship of Jesus Christ and the church. This covenant promises solidarity between husband and wife. More than a contract, which depends on the fulfillment of certain conditions (a quid pro quo), a covenant is unconditional, freely given, and is intended to last forever. It is the way in which Christ loves the church, dying for humanity, so that all people may be united with him some day. The sacrament of marriage, with its covenantal agreement between husband and wife, provides a glimpse of the relationship of Christ and the church. Finally, the sacrament of confirmation is rooted in the promise of Jesus to send an advocate, the Paraclete, a manifestation of the Holy Spirit, to empower his followers to continue his ministry and expand the body of Christ. Thus, finding their roots in Jesus' teaching and work, we can say that the sacraments are instituted by Christ.

Third, the sacraments have been entrusted to the church. Accordingly, as the *Catechism* explains, the Roman Catholic

Church renders Christ present through its continual celebration of the sacraments. These efficacious signs, practiced faithfully, reveal the presence of Christ in our midst. This revelation of Christ's presence in the church is why the church is called "the body of Christ," because here Christ is embodied. The church extends his presence, visibly, orally, tangibly, continuing his ministry on earth. In a sense, the church becomes the face, voice, and hands of Christ. It is through our activity in the world that the world sees, hears, and feels Christ. This activity includes all of our teaching and preaching, care of the sick and the sinner, and pointing to Christ's presence revealed in the special moments of our lives, from funerals to festivals.

The Celebration of the Sacraments Is a Fruitful Celebration

Referring back to the *Catechism*'s definition of a sacrament, we should consider two more terms, namely, the "visible rites by which the sacraments are celebrated" and the notion that they "bear fruit" in those with the required dispositions.

Some sacraments—but not all—require material objects, such as bread and wine for the Eucharist, water for baptism, or oil for the infirmed in the anointing of the sick. Bread and

wine are served and shared in a meal. Baptismal water is used
for washing, refreshing body and soul with new life. Oil is used
for anointing, signifying a person's membership in the Christian
community. The fact that Christians celebrate these rites indicates that they are social, rather than solitary, events. In other
words, they provide occasions for the community to gather, and
in the gathering Christ is made present, recalling his words,
"When two or three are gathered in my name, there I am in
the midst of them" (Matt. 18:20 RSV). We are supposed to celebrate sacraments with others, not by ourselves. The visible
unity of the assembled church, gathered in his name, manifests
the presence of Christ on earth. "So that they may all be one, as
you, Father, are in me and I am in you, that they also may be in
us" (Jn. 17:21 NAB).

Finally, the effectiveness of any sacrament will be shown
through its "fruitfulness," that is, the fruit born by the worshiping
community. Such a statement indicates that we are concerned
with more than executing the rite properly and following all
the rubrics with precision. To be sure, rubrics are important,
and we should follow them. But our faithful adherence to the
rubrics themselves does not in and of itself make for a fruitful
sacrament.

Nevertheless, most people value precision and excellence—
and for good reasons. When we watch different productions of

Hamlet, for instance, it is sometimes clear which is done with proper execution and which is not. If Kenneth Branagh plays the lead role, we know what we will get, as opposed to, say, a high school sophomore. The student will have memorized his lines and may recite them flawlessly, but he lacks the experience of the seasoned professional who better understands both the text as well as the human condition, which he depicts.

When it comes to performing sacraments, precision is also important. There is a "validity" to a worship service, citing the principle of *ex opere operato,* that comes simply from performing the rite correctly. Translated literally as "by the work, worked," the principle of *ex opere operato* assures the worshiping community that so long as the ritual is celebrated according to the rubrics, then it is effective and God's grace will be conveyed. This is especially important when faced with a minister whose fidelity to the church or whose moral integrity may be questionable. The recent spate of scandals among the clergy gives us cause to consider this principle. Imagine, for example, a situation in which an infant is baptized by a priest who is later charged with the abuse of a minor. The family may wonder if their child was in fact truly baptized: Did the fact that the priest was later found guilty of a heinous crime and a serious sin render the sacrament meaningless or invalid? The answer is very clearly no. The validity of the sacrament does not rely

on the worthiness of the minister but on the proper celebration
of the ritual. This is because the church believes that Christ is
the true high priest for all worship, while the ordained minister
mediates the presence of Christ in a particular way.

However, we should still distinguish between what is valid
and what is fruitful. Validity concerns the minimal requirements. But fruitfulness considers the effect worship has on
the community, which is shown by the difference it makes in
the lives of the community members. To illustrate, consider
Jesus' miracle healings, which the one healed follows with a
response. In many cases, the person, once freed from his or her
malady, follows the Lord. Such an encounter with Jesus follows
a pattern of call and response; the Lord calls and the person
responds. Christian worship follows this pattern as well. Each
celebration provides a special opportunity to encounter Christ:
the Lord calls to his people, and they respond by following him
in prayer and in public action. This lived response in daily life
indicates the fruitfulness of the sacrament and points to Christ's
presence in the world. As Scripture attests: "By their fruits you
will know them" (Matt. 7:16 NAB).

The distinction between validity and fruitfulness is clear
in the Hebrew prophets as well. For example, Amos rails
against those who offer elaborate worship to God while
ignoring their neighbors. "I hate, I spurn your feasts, I take

no pleasure in your solemnities. . . . Away with your noisy songs! I will not listen to the melodies of your harps. But if you would offer me holocausts, then let justice surge like water, and goodness like an unfailing stream" (5:21–24 NAB). Likewise, Hosea chastises the Israelites by declaring in the name of God, "For it is love that I desire, not sacrifice, and knowledge of God rather than holocausts" (6:6 NAB). Moving into the New Testament, Saint Paul echoes the warning of the prophets when he criticizes the Corinthians for the way they celebrate the Eucharist. He is disgusted with their divisiveness around the banquet table of unity. In his words, "When you assemble as a church, I hear that there are divisions among you, and to a degree I believe it. . . . When you meet in one place, then, it is not to eat the Lord's supper, for in eating, each one goes ahead with his own supper, and one goes hungry while another gets drunk. . . . You show contempt for the church of God and make those who have nothing feel ashamed" (1 Cor. 11:18–22 NAB).[10]

This is the reason why the definition of sacraments taken from the *Catechism* concludes by mentioning "required dispositions." Again, entering into the sacraments entails more than receiving divine grace; Christians are invited to respond to the divine call. As a result, one's disposition plays an important part in worship. It is the anticipation of meeting the Lord coupled with a willingness to be transformed more fully into the body of Christ. According to Saint Augustine, in preparing to receive the Lord's body and blood, "we place ourselves on the paten." In the "Spiritual Exercises," Saint Ignatius of Loyola recommends that one cultivate an appropriate disposition for prayer by imagining that one is about to meet the king of the land.[11] Ignatius has the reader consider how he would comport himself and be aware of his speech, his actions, and his appearance. Having the proper disposition before the Lord promotes awareness, allowing one to focus more clearly on the event, and then to receive the Lord and to respond wholeheartedly.

Venturing onto the Dark Side

So far, we have been discussing how the sacramental principle is the basis for our claim that "everything is sacred." Some, however, may protest that such a claim ignores the darker side of humanity and of the world. Given the state of the world as we know it—the carnage of war; the plight of poverty in developing lands; plague and famine; the illegal trafficking of weapons, narcotics, and humans—can anyone claim that everything is sacred?

Clearly, we confront here the darkness to which John refers in his prologue. This darkness has indeed overcome many people throughout history, and the current era is no exception. How does such darkness coexist with the idea that everything is somehow sacred? All of these dark, evil, disappointing, or disastrous things distort the reality of God's creation.

Christianity presents the world with a paradox—we view the cross as a sign of hope. The very instrument used as the cruelest form of capital punishment ever devised stands in every church as a symbol of salvation and a reminder that God has conquered death. A dark event provides a ray of light. Christians pray *through* the cross, not around it or despite it. Following Jesus' command, his disciples embrace the cross: "If anyone wishes to come after me, he must deny himself, take up his cross daily and follow me" (Lk. 9:23 NAB). In doing so, Christians follow Jesus through his sorrowful passion and death, to share in his glorious resurrection. Christians mark their worship by signing themselves with the cross.

On Good Friday, Christians stand in procession to venerate the cross with a touch or a kiss. This is not masochistic behavior. Christians do not worship the cross in itself but because of what Christ accomplished through it. On Calvary Jesus could embrace the cross because he believed that this was the will of his Father and that his embrace of it would ultimately unite him with his Father. Through tragedy came beauty.

To believe that everything is sacred is not to suggest that we live in a perfect world, as if we could ignore the ugly part of life and focus on the nicer parts. Such an attitude may be reinforced by a popular culture that confuses beauty with that which is pretty, attractive, and pleasant to behold. The sacred refers not to that which is perfect but to that which is perfectible; it refers to the belief that creation is ongoing and that God continues to create in our lifetime. As we read from the prophet Isaiah: "See I am doing something new! Now it springs forth; do you not perceive it?" (Isa. 43:19 NAB). The evil experienced within the world, when embraced like Jesus embracing the cross, may be transformed into something glorious for God. Again, confronting evil is not masochistic behavior but is a way to shine light into darkness and an opportunity to recognize the presence of the divine within the mundane. Rather than acquiesce and accept the way of the world as the fate of humanity, Christians recognize how humans have altered the world and seek to restore God's creation. The world itself is not dark but it has been darkened by sin.

Have you ever had an opportunity to visit the Vatican and see the Sistine Chapel? If you did more than twenty years ago, you were gazing at the famous ceiling in a darkened state. Through the centuries, Michelangelo's masterpiece grew dark from an accumulation of dirt. Many artists believed that this was the actual color tone the painter used. Such thinking promoted theories that this work was a part of Michelangelo's "dark period," and so he employed darker colors in his work. But then it was cleaned, and after the cleaning, the world realized that the darkened ceiling was not the way the artist intended it at all; rather, it was the accumulated effect of humanity paying homage to a legendary work and the gradual weathering of the material. The restored work is magnificent, the colors glow brightly, and the public's appreciation for this master has been renewed. Someone had the idea to clean the masterpiece, in a sense, shining a light into darkness.

The divine act of shining a light into darkness restores our view of the world and of ourselves. This view has been marred by generations of sinful discoloration, darkening the creation. Aided by the divine light, we can see the world as God sees it, and look at ourselves through God's eyes.

Of course those who restored the ceiling of the Sistine Chapel needed an image to guide them to their goal; they believed that they were restoring a great work of art. They had to envision what the finished project would look like. They needed some sense of where they were going before they could begin their work. With the goal carefully laid out, they began their work, a movement from darkness to light. In a similar way, sacraments provide a liminal experience as we move from one state to another. We seek the divine through the mundane; the ordinary leads to the extraordinary. The work of transforming the evil we witness is the attempt to restore what has been lost in the belief that God's work waits to be revealed in a new way. "Behold I am making something new!" Indeed, all the world is charged with the grandeur of God. For this reason we can say, "everything is sacred."

And it all begins with what? Baptism.

baptism forms character

Fiunt non nascuntur Christiani
Christians are made, not born.
—Tertullian[12]

The word *sacrament* is derived from a Latin noun, *sacramentum*, which originally referred to an initiation ritual practiced by the Roman military. Standing in a public ceremony, the recruits would pledge their fidelity to the gods of Rome and to their commanding officer. Then they would be branded or tattooed with the seal of Rome—SPQR (*Senatus Populusque Romanus*, or "For the senate and people of Rome")—and with the insignia of their regiment. For all intents and purposes, this mark was permanent. This seal would indicate that this man was a soldier of the Roman army and entitled to all the privileges of a soldier. Also, should he ever desert his company he could be caught and brought back for punishment. This Roman seal gave notice of who this man was in relation to the greater community. In a sense, the seal indicated who he was as well as *whose* he was. The soldier trained for special service within the empire, and in return the empire pledged its support for him.[13]

So how did this word come to be associated with the Christian practice of initiation? In the second century, Christianity was still considered to be an illegal cult, viewed suspiciously by the people of the empire. Vicious rumors abounded about Christians. They were considered cannibals since they were said to consume the body and blood of their leader. They were thought to be criminals since they worshiped a convicted criminal, Jesus of Nazareth, who everyone knew was executed by the empire. And they were accused of being homosexuals due to stories of their sharing a "kiss of peace," in which men kissed men and women kissed women. Such rumors kept Christians on the margins of the empire.

Faced with this sort of opposition, they sought to explain themselves—their rites and beliefs—to demonstrate that they could live in harmony within the Roman Empire while honoring their Lord and Savior, Jesus Christ. They did not intend any threat against Caesar; they did not intend to undermine Rome.

However, as true disciples of Jesus Christ, they considered it their mission to spread the Word of God to the ends of the earth. We find the command for this mission in the conclusion of the Gospel of Matthew: "Go, therefore, and make disciples of all nations, baptizing them in the name of the Father, and of the Son, and of the Holy Spirit, teaching them to observe all that I have commanded you" (Matt. 28:19–20 NAB). There it is, right there: baptism was clear and simple. Christ gave his followers an explicit command to carry out this work. But how could they explain the purpose of baptism in a way that a Roman pagan[14] could understand? The last thing they wanted was to once again be misunderstood.

This is probably the primary reason why several Christian writers at the time described baptism as similar to the Roman ritual for military recruits, the *sacramentum*. They made a clear correlation with the soldier's pledge and the brand he received. Just as the soldier pledged his fidelity to the gods of Rome and to his commanding officer, the "neophytes," or those to be baptized, pledged their fidelity to Jesus Christ, the Son of God, and to the community of Christians. In turn, the community pledged its support of its new members. Then the neophytes were "branded," that is to say, they were marked with an invisible and indelible seal, claiming them as Christians and to be recognized as such by the community of Christ's disciples.

Saint John Chrysostom, a "doctor of the church," described this seal in a Lenten instruction on baptism. Writing in the year 390, he said,

> Then once you have . . . confessed his sovereignty over you and pronounced the words by which you pledge yourself to Christ, you are now a soldier and have signed on for a spiritual contest. Accordingly the bishop anoints you on the forehead with spiritual myron, placing a seal on your head and saying: N. is anointed in the name of the Father, the Son and the Holy Spirit.[15]

Note here that there is a play on the word "seal." In one sense, a seal indicates ownership and authority, as when the president of the United States affixes the seal of his office to a document. Then this document is given special recognition, as we know that it comes from his office. Likewise, ranchers brand their cattle to show their ownership of these animals. In this way, a seal can indicate ownership and authority.

We also talk of a "seal" as a device for protection. A homeowner seals the space around the windows to protect the house from drafts. We seal our leftovers in a plastic bag to preserve them against bacteria. In this way a seal protects. The baptismal seal serves a dual purpose. On the one hand, it indicates ownership, or perhaps it would be better to say membership, as the newly baptized are made members of the Christian community. They are recognized as sons and daughters of God, and they now belong to this community. We know who they are, and *whose* they are. On the other hand, baptism offers a seal of protection against the power of evil. This is not a magic spell promising that no harm will come to us. We are simply assured that God's grace will overpower the evil we will encounter.[16]

In the ancient church, the baptized demonstrated a turn away from evil and toward good by physically turning to the west, renouncing evil. This is the direction of sunset, signifying the coming darkness associated with sin and death. In the second question the minister asks, "Do you reject the glamour of evil?" In an Easter homily, Pope Benedict XVI explained that evil's glamour refers to "the splendor of the ancient cult of the gods and of the ancient theatre in which it was entertaining to watch people being torn limb from limb by wild beasts." We can imagine the spectacle of the gladiators in the Coliseum. So one renounces a culture that entraps people in the adoration of temporal power and the cruelty it fosters.[17] By asserting three times their rejection of Satan, they express a desire for "conversion," literally a turning around. So now they turn toward the east, the direction of sunrise. They make a threefold profession of faith, confessing their belief in God the Father, the Creator; in Jesus Christ, the Son of God; and in the Holy Spirit.

The turn from left to right (from west to east) is symbolic because it signals a reorientation of one's life. Grace enters and moves the person to change course in order to follow Christ. The newly baptized resemble the disciples who, upon hearing the call from Jesus to drop everything and follow him (Matt. 4:18–22), change the direction of their lives. They drop their nets, the sign of their livelihood as fishermen, and take up a new life with Jesus, who has promised to make them "fishers of men." This reorientation is a recurring theme throughout the New Testament. Consider John the Baptist proclaiming in the desert, "Repent, for the kingdom of heaven is at hand" (Matt. 3:1–2 NAB). The cry for repentance calls for a change of heart and conduct, turning one's life from rebellion to obedience toward God. The word *repentance*, we said, implies a change of heart as well as a change in the direction of one's life. This is the first step of expressing Christian faith, as we hear from Saint Paul: "I preached the need to repent and turn to God, and to do works giving evidence of repentance" (Acts 26:20 NAB). This conversion is, as Richard McBrien explains, "The fundamental change of heart (metanoia) by which one accepts Jesus as the Christ and orients his whole life around Christ and the Kingdom of God."[18]

In a sense, baptism reorients one's life, turning a person around to face another direction and walk along a new pathway. This reorientation has been rendered clearly in the design of many cathedrals. For example, at the new Cathedral of Christ the Light in Oakland, California, worshipers approach the building from the street level by walking along the "pilgrim's path," a straight walkway with a slight incline to the entrance. Passing through the grand doorway, they continue walking straight to the baptismal pool. But upon walking around the pool, one must change direction at an angle of forty-five degrees to follow the aisle through the nave to the sanctuary. The architect's design expresses the reorientation of the Christian's life through baptism.

Like the first disciples, the newly baptized change direction to follow Christ. We could carry the metaphor of orientation further and claim that baptism may even serve to *disorient* the disciples of Jesus Christ. To take baptism seriously—to profess the creed earnestly—may cause confusion because Christianity inverts the customs and the moral standards of the culture. For we are baptized into the death and resurrection of Jesus Christ, following the way of the cross through Gethsemane and Calvary, to the empty garden tomb. As alluded to earlier, Saint Paul describes this cross as a "scandal." The passion of the Lord confounds common sense and good judgment; it is only rendered intelligible through an appreciation of God's great love for humanity. The cross disorients people from their natural paths of daily living. Paul experienced the scandal of the cross and its disorienting effect firsthand through his own conversion, being thrown to the ground and blinded for three days, with the piercing voice from heaven calling to him to turn around (Acts 9:1–9). He underwent a radical reorientation, and his life ended by dying for his belief in Jesus Christ, the Son of God—the very thing for which he had had others executed. Of course, not all are capable of surrendering themselves to such a reorientation. Consider the gospel story of the rich man who goes out of his way to meet Jesus and declares his interest in attaining salvation (Lk. 18:18–25). Jesus asks him if he observes the commandments. The man seems to have mastered the first stage of salvation, that of observing the commandments. But when Jesus calls him—challenges him—to live a different lifestyle, unencumbered by material goods and free to follow his personal quest of salvation, the man turns and walks away. Because this new direction is so disorienting to the rich man, he turns away from Jesus. In baptism, the turning from west to east, rejecting Satan, and accepting Christ symbolizes the radical reorientation of one's life in conformity with Christ.

Christians will continue to be tempted, and they will suffer the slings and arrows of the human condition. This is to say they will suffer from the effects of sinfulness. The forgiveness of sin played an important part of Jesus' ministry. He devoted much time to forgiving the sins of people he met along his path. And after the resurrection, when he returned to his disciples, he gave them the charge, "Receive the Holy Spirit. If you forgive the sins of any, they are forgiven; if you retain the sins of any, they are retained" (Jn. 20:22–23 RSV). Today the followers of Jesus Christ continue his ministry, professing a readiness to forgive as well as to receive forgiveness, as we pray in the "Lord's Prayer," "Forgive us our sins (trespasses, debts) as we forgive those who have sinned against us."

According to the *Catechism of the Catholic Church* (no. 997), baptism is the chief sacrament for the forgiveness of sins because it unites us with Christ, who died for our sins and won our salvation. Baptism seals us by cleansing us of original sin. But some may wonder, if baptism is truly effective, why do the baptized continue to sin? To answer this question, let us first consider the meaning of the word *sin*.

The root of the word *sin* is *hamartia*, which means to "miss the mark." The meaning implies that a person recognizes the "mark" but for some reason could not reach it. Picture an archer holding his bow and arrow, aiming at a target. With the bull's-eye in plain sight, he draws his bow and prepares to shoot. His aim is clear. But suddenly he is distracted by a loud noise coming from the side. He flinches, lets the arrow fly, but completely misses the target. He knew his mark and ordinarily he would be able to hit it, but because of a distraction, he missed the mark.

Sin is essentially a distraction—the distraction from the way we want to go. We know what is right and good, but sometimes we get distracted; we are enticed by evil and lose our way. Despite our ability to recognize what is good, we choose evil. All of this is a matter of "personal sin," the acts for which we are morally responsible. We distinguish personal sin from original sin, the sin with which we are born. Original sin addresses the belief that human beings have lost something from the way we were created by God and recognizes that we are unduly influenced by the evil spirit. Because we are made in the image and likeness of God, we are essentially good. But we are not perfect. The divine image has been tainted, and we are drawn toward sin. In a word, we suffer from "concupiscence," the inclination to evil. We suffer from a tendency toward distraction. Baptism erases original sin and, by the grace of Jesus Christ, directs us back to God. To be sure, Christians live in an ongoing spiritual struggle, lured by concupiscence yet destined for salvation. The promise made and received in faith is that evil will not have the last word. God will be victorious.

a brief history of baptism

The Baptism of Jesus

> I baptize you with water . . . he will baptize you with the
> Holy Spirit. (Lk. 3:16 RSV)

To understand the history of Christian baptism, we must
first look at the four Gospels and the Letters of Saint Paul.
Here we find three important themes. First, there is the story
of the baptism of Jesus in the Jordan River, one of those rare
events that is documented in all four of the Gospels. For each
of the Gospel writers, this story introduces Jesus to the reader.
Second, baptism serves as a metaphor for the coming passion of
Jesus Christ, a dying to sin and a rising to new life. Third, Jesus'
final instruction to his disciples centers on the importance of

continuing the ministry of baptism. The disciples follow this command in the book of the Acts of the Apostles as well.

We first meet John the Baptist in the Gospel stories of Jesus' baptism. John practiced his ritual of baptism by the Jordan River in the wilderness of Judea. Not much is known about John's formation as a prophet. He probably had contact with the Qumran community. This community became well known in 1947 with the discovery of its ancient writings, "the Dead Sea Scrolls," which shed much light on the period of history in which Jesus lived. In the excavation of this site, researchers discovered that this community engineered a vast and complex system for collecting water, which included several small pools used for bathing and perhaps ritual baptism.

John practiced an ascetic lifestyle. According to the Gospel of Matthew (3:1–4), his food was locusts and wild honey, and his appearance—a garment of camel's hair and a leather girdle—resembles that of the prophet Elijah: "He wore a garment of haircloth, with a girdle of leather about his loins. It is Elijah the Tishbite" (2 Kgs. 1:8 RSV). John's mission was to proclaim repentance, which literally means "turning," that is, a turning away from sin and turning toward a proper life. His advice to those who asked about the way of salvation was to direct them to live justly. In his word, "He who has two coats, let him share with him who has none; and he who has food, let him do likewise." To tax collectors he advised, "Collect no more than is appointed you." And to soldiers he said, "Rob no one by violence or by false accusation, and be content with your wages" (Lk. 3:10–14 RSV). John's advice was to turn away from greed, selfishness, and violence, and turn toward a life of compassion and justice.

John's message reinforced the Jewish understanding of repentance. For the Jews, repentance included a need for sacrifice in which they made an offering to atone for their offensive behavior. For example, the book of Leviticus prescribes that in the case of someone who has committed a grievous fault against the Lord, "He shall bring as a guilt offering to the priest an unblemished ram of the flock of the established value. The priest shall then make atonement for the fault . . . and it will be forgiven. Such is the offering for guilt; the penalty of the guilt must be paid to the Lord" (Lev. 5:18–19 NAB). However, both the prophets and the testimony of John made it clear that these offerings would not automatically grant atonement to a sinner. Rather, genuine contrition—that is to say, a change of heart—was necessary for forgiveness.

The roots of Christian baptism are found in the Hebrew theme of purification carried throughout the Pentateuch.[19] Ritual washings were commonplace for devout Jews. A New

Testament example for this can be found in the story of the wedding at Cana (Jn. 2:1–11), in which the Evangelist John references the six stone water jars to be used for the Jewish rites of purification. The purpose of these rites was ceremonial rather than hygienic. John the Baptist (like Jesus) emerges from this Hebrew tradition, appearing on the shores of the Jordan River and calling people to repentance for their sins.

When John the Baptist said, "I baptize you with water . . . he will baptize you with the Holy Spirit" (Lk. 3:16 RSV), he was already showing a shift in the purpose of baptism, from water to the Spirit, from purification to inspiration. With the baptism of Jesus, it is clear that more is happening than the cleansing of sin. All four Gospels at this moment describe a theophany, a manifestation of the triune God. As we read in the Gospel of Mark: "When (Jesus) came up out of the water, immediately he saw the heavens opened and the Spirit descending upon him like a dove; and a voice came from heaven, 'You are my beloved Son; with you I am well pleased'" (Mk. 1:9–11 RSV). Each of the Gospels describes the Spirit descending upon Jesus like a dove and records a pronouncement that Jesus is the Son of God. In the synoptic Gospels, Matthew, Mark, and Luke, a voice from heaven speaks; in the Gospel of John, it is the Baptist who bears witness to Jesus' relationship with the Father. So, the text of all four Gospels notes the presence of the Trinity at Jesus' baptism: the Father reveals the Son, and the Spirit rests with him.[20]

There is some variation of detail in the four accounts of this story. In Mark and Matthew, Jesus descends into the water and is baptized by John. He then emerges from the water and we hear a voice from heaven. In Luke, just before Jesus is baptized, we learn that John has been arrested by King Herod (Lk. 3:19–20), suggesting that John did not baptize Jesus. Still, Jesus emerges from the river and the heavenly voice speaks. Then, in John, we find no indication of Jesus stepping into the river and being immersed in the water, but we hear the same pronouncement about Jesus, this time by John the Baptist. So the four Evangelists vary concerning who baptizes Jesus, how he is baptized, and who speaks to reveal the relationship of Father and Son. However, they all agree that this baptism is more than a ritual purification. It is an opening and an opportunity to receive the Holy Spirit. The Baptist's description of himself makes it clear, as does the presence of the Spirit in the form of a dove. New meaning is given to this ritual bath.

One question that arises here is why Jesus descended into the water. Why did Jesus lower himself—literally and figuratively—to receive baptism? If the purpose of John's baptism in the Jordan was for a cleansing from spiritual impurity, what purpose would it serve for Jesus? In short, did Jesus *need* baptism?

On the one hand, baptism was not necessary for Jesus since he committed no sin and he bore no personal guilt from sinfulness. Matthew's account broaches this question. When Jesus approaches John to be baptized by him, John tries to prevent him, saying, "I need to be baptized by you, and do you come to me?" But Jesus answers, "Let it be so now, for thus it is fitting for us to fulfill all righteousness" (Matt. 3:13–15 RSV). This dialogue appears in Matthew's Gospel only.

Some believe that the baptism of Jesus was a source of embarrassment to the early church. They would have seen it as a humiliation for the Son of God to be baptized just like a sinner. For this reason, Luke omits John the Baptist from the scene, and John does not mention the actual baptism. It is embarrassing to hear of Jesus' submitting himself to John for baptism when Jesus' baptism was superior to that of John, and because John described his own as a baptism of repentance, perhaps calling into question Jesus' sinlessness. Clearly Jesus stood before John, innocent of any sinful action, making baptism seem unnecessary.

On the other hand, while Jesus committed no sin, he did carry with him the sins of humanity, bearing upon himself the guilt of the world. This is no empty gesture on Jesus' part. He bore the pain of human failing just as a parent bears the shame caused by the criminal behavior of a son or daughter. While the parents themselves are not guilty of any crime, they feel, in an acute way, the suffering of other people caused by their child. The Scripture scholar John McKenzie writes, "In submitting to baptism by John the Baptist, Jesus did not confess that he was a sinner, but openly signified his real union with sinful humanity, which he had come to redeem from its sins."[21] Karl Barth likewise opines that no one was in greater need of baptism that day at the Jordan than Jesus, who was weighed down with the sins of the world.[22] In this way, Jesus' baptism foreshadows his crucifixion. Here Jesus assumes the role of the scapegoat, one who bears the blame for others and suffers in their place. For the Hebrew people the scapegoat was literally a goat upon whom a high priest symbolically laid the sins of the people. The book of Leviticus describes the rubrics for celebrating the annual Day of Atonement like this.

Aaron shall lay both his hands upon the head of the live goat, and confess over him all the iniquities of the people of Israel, and all their transgressions, all their sins; and he shall put them upon the head of the goat, and send him away into the wilderness. . . . The goat shall bear all their iniquities upon him to a solitary land; and he shall let the goat go in the wilderness. (Lev. 16:21–22 RSV)

By carrying the sins of the people into the desert, the scapegoat bore away the stain of evil from the people. The early Latin translation of the Bible, the Vulgate, referred to this animal as the *caper emisaarrius*, from which is derived the English word *escape goat* or *scapegoat*.[23] Peter compares Jesus to a scapegoat when he writes: "He himself bore our sins in his body on the tree, that we might die to sin and live to righteousness. By his wounds you have been healed" (1 Pet. 2:24).

The crucifixion on Calvary, and the notion of Jesus' bearing our sins in his body, returns us to the baptism at the Jordan. Both events proved embarrassing. Just as some in the early church were disturbed by the thought of Jesus' being baptized by a man, the brutal death of Jesus Christ proved scandalous to many as well. Saint Paul refers to the *skandalon* ("scandal") of the cross; indeed, why would God endure such humiliation for humanity?

Jesus suffered such agony on the cross in expiation for the sins of humanity, that is, to remove the darkness of sin and to restore humanity to the image God had created. For this reason, God raised him in glory. He also begins his mission on earth with his baptism, bearing the burden of sin, descending into the water, a symbolic death and the washing away of sin, and he hears the voice of the Father calling to him, "My beloved." He is beloved because he is obedient to the Father, who expresses his love for humankind through the forgiveness of sin.

Baptism Is a Metaphor for Salvation

> Jesus said to them, "You do not know what you are asking. Are you able to drink the cup that I drink, or to be baptized with the baptism with which I am baptized?" (Mk. 10:38 RSV)

Understanding Jesus as the scapegoat teaches us that baptism entails a dying to oneself. To be baptized means to share in the passion of Jesus Christ, a reality the disciples were slow to grasp.

The Gospel of Mark alludes to the ignorance of the disciples as they ask Jesus for seats of honor when they reach his kingdom (10:37). The disciples must first learn "the way" to the kingdom, and that way passes through a period of turmoil. The Gospel of Luke provides a similar warning: "I came to cast fire upon the earth; and would that it were already kindled! I have a baptism to be baptized with; and how I am constrained until it is accomplished! Do you think that I have come to give peace on earth? No, I tell you, but rather division" (Lk. 12:49–51 RSV). Jesus goes on to describe divisions through the metaphor of a family in which the members stand against one another. To follow Jesus often meant that one's family would be left behind.

Thirty or forty years later, when the Gospels were first written, baptized Christians very often still faced this tension between their lives at home and their lives of faith. Christians were viewed as members of a strange cult and often found themselves ostracized from their families and regarded with suspicion by the community.

Baptism always requires a dying to oneself so that one may rise to new life. Sometimes this meant leaving one's family behind. This new life, though, is always demonstrated within a renewed relationship with God and with the community. Of this Paul writes: "You were washed, you were sanctified, you were justified in the name of the Lord Jesus Christ and in the Spirit of our God" (1 Cor. 6:11 RSV). Likewise, Titus and Peter proclaim that the baptized are made "righteous" by Christ.[24] All of this signals a new relationship between the baptized person and God. This new relationship is the meaning of "justification," which means to stand in right relationship with God. Because of sin, that relationship was broken; while God remains constant and never turns away from humanity, a person who is distracted by temptation wanders away from God. Baptism washes away the effects of that sin brought on by temptation and restores the relationship. Now the person and God are properly aligned.

To illustrate this notion of justification, imagine that you are working on a document on your computer and you need to "justify the margin." You have probably done this before. By a simple click, you can change the right margin from a ragged edge to one of alignment, forming a straight line similar to the left margin. You have thereby "justified" it. Well, justification in a theological sense is also a matter of proper alignment. Theologically speaking, a person is justified when she or he is restored to a right relationship with God or, in other words, when one is properly aligned with God.

Justification also means that the baptized stand in a new relationship with the community of believers. They are incorporated into the body of Christ and become members of one body, functioning together as a living organism. Paul compares the body of Christ to the human body and its intrinsic need for harmony.

> For just as the body is one and has many members, and all the members of the body, though many, are one body, so it is with Christ. . . . God has so composed the body . . . that there may be no discord in the body, but that the members may have the same care for one another. (1 Cor. 12:12, 24–25 RSV)

Imagine how ludicrous it would be for a person's head to choose to ignore the feet. These body parts must work together for the whole body to function properly. Similarly, the members of the Christian community must work together in harmony for the body of Christ to carry on its mission. Some may wonder how the notion of working together applies to infants after their baptism since they are not yet capable of making such a choice. For them it is a matter of being raised in the Christian community, by which they come to experience life within this body and reap the rewards of mutual cooperation in the name of Jesus Christ. Eventually, it is hoped, they will choose for themselves to follow Christ through the church.

Any barriers erected by cultural distinctions are washed away. As Paul writes: "For as many of you as were baptized into Christ have put on Christ. There is neither Jew nor Greek, there is neither slave nor free, there is neither male nor female; for you are all one in Christ Jesus" (Gal. 3:27–28 RSV). The Christian community strives for harmony, that is, all members working together for the common goal of incorporating the body of Christ on earth and directing all humanity to the eternal kingdom of God. Paul, in the quotation above, seems to echo Jesus' prayer for the disciples in his "final discourse": "Father, keep them in your name, which you have given me, that they may be one, even as we are one" (Jn. 17:11). The unified Christian community is a sign of Christ's continued presence on earth.

A Command to Baptize

The third stage in this brief history of baptism begins right here: when Jesus Christ commands his followers to baptize. Simply put, our Lord tells us to baptize others in his name.

Having been incorporated into the body of Christ, the baptized join the church's mission to evangelize; they spread the faith and bring others into the fold. The Christian community is no mere club established solely for the benefit of its members. Rather, the church has been established by Christ to spread his name throughout the world. The church will grow through baptism, and Christians express their obedience to the Lord through baptism.

Shortly after their encounter with the Lord, when the disciples hear the command to baptize in Jesus' name, Peter finds himself directing a crowd of people to have themselves baptized. Peter stands on a balcony outside the upper room where the disciples have been celebrating secretly the feast of Pentecost. Inspired by the Holy Spirit, he preaches to the crowds of Jerusalem and wins their hearts. Responding to his words, they shout to him and the disciples, "What shall we do?" Peter tells them, "Repent, and be baptized every one of you, in the name of Jesus Christ" (Acts 2:37–38 RSV). The disciples remained faithful to this command to baptize.

Jesus clearly states to Nicodemus the necessity of baptism
for salvation: "Unless one is born of water and the Spirit, he
cannot enter the kingdom of God" (Jn. 3:5 ESV). For the early
church, baptism was an essential step for salvation. However,
later on this seems to have become a problematic issue, when
the church became concerned with infant mortality, raising the
question of what happens to innocent souls who are not guilty
of sin yet have never been baptized because they died at a
young age. Can they too enter the heavenly kingdom? (We will
come back to this topic later, in the discussion of limbo.)

Now, you might ask, did Jesus ever baptize anyone? We find
conflicting messages in the Gospel of John. First we read, "Jesus
and his disciples went into the land of Judea; there he remained
with them and baptized" (3:22 RSV). A parenthetical statement
follows, however: "although Jesus himself did not baptize, but
only his disciples" (4:2 RSV). According to the Scripture scholar
Pheme Perkins, "A parenthetical comment has been added to
dispel the impression that Jesus had baptized people in imitation
of John the Baptist."[25] Following the Scripture then, we cannot
say that Jesus baptized anyone. While we know that he accompanied his disciples into the land of Judea, where they performed
baptism, there is no way to be sure that Jesus baptized.

What did the ritual of baptism look and sound like? How did
the disciples baptize those who wanted to follow Christ, and

what did they say to them? In reading the New Testament, we actually find little information about these things. We do learn that almost everyone who accepted Christianity was baptized (Acts 2:37–41), and the great majority of those baptized were adults, although we can presume some children were included as part of a household (Acts 11:14; 16:15, 33).

We read of individuals being submerged in a body of water and having the name of Jesus conferred upon them. They were immersed, like Jesus was, about whom we read, that he came out of the water (Mk. 1:10; Matt. 3:16). We also read of Philip baptizing a eunuch who "went down into the water" (Acts 8:38 RSV). The practice of immersion provides a metaphor for the belief that, through baptism, the Christian dies and rises to new life. "You were buried with him in baptism, in which you were also raised with him through faith in the working of God, who raised him from the dead" (Col. 2:12 RSV).[26] However, because the New Testament lacks a specific description about how baptisms were performed, other practices such as sprinkling developed. This change may have come about to simplify the ceremony, since it takes much longer to immerse the candidates than to pour water over them. It may also have been influenced by architecture: a church could conserve space by building a baptismal font instead of a pool. The change to sprinkling become predominant in the Middle Ages and continues to be widely practiced today. Sprinkling is certainly a valid form of baptism. Sometimes it is necessary as, for example, when a person is incapacitated and cannot enter the pool. However, we need to consider the sign value of how submersion or immersion dramatically visualizes the descent into a watery tomb: the dying to oneself and rising into new life. Indeed, the Roman Catholic Church encourages this practice: "Immersion . . . is more suitable as a symbol of participation in the death and resurrection of Jesus Christ."[27] This symbolism is no small matter. The baptismal pool represents the tomb in which Jesus Christ was buried on Good Friday. In this watery tomb, one dies with Christ in order to be reborn in the glory of God. The pool then also represents the womb, which provides rebirth. So the pool symbolizes both tomb and womb. The act of fully immersing oneself leaves the person soaking wet, indicating that the neophyte has been washed clean, the way we feel after a refreshing shower. The simpler practice of sprinkling may suggest the symbolism of death and rebirth, or it may focus more on spiritual cleansing. To be sure, baptism does produce a spiritual cleansing, but that cleansing occurs through dying to oneself.

The words spoken in baptism originally focused on the conferral of the name of Jesus, meaning that the newly baptized received the name of their Savior. For example, we read in the

Acts of the Apostles Peter's instruction to the crowd on Pentecost, "Repent, and be baptized every one of you, in the name of Jesus Christ" (Acts 2:38 RSV). Receiving the name of Jesus means that one submits to the claims of the Christ and to the community that accepts Jesus as its founder.[28] However, as this formula of baptism evolved during the time of the early church, the Trinitarian name of God replaced the name of Jesus. Recall the command given by Jesus to his disciples to baptize "in the name of the Father and of the Son and of the Holy Spirit" (Mt. 28:19 RSV). It is arguable as to whether these are the actual words (the *ipsissima verba*) of Jesus to his disciples before departing from them. Nevertheless, the use of the Trinitarian name became the practice for Christian baptism. We will take up this topic later.

The Practice of Baptism in the Early Church

It is probably already becoming clear to you that whenever Christians gather around the baptismal font to initiate a new member into the community of faith, they are carrying out an ancient tradition, following the customs of their ancestors. In fact, we have documents from the early church that describe in some detail the proper procedure for baptism. One of the earliest of these documents is known by the unusual title the *Didache*, or the "Teaching of the Lord to the Gentiles Through the Apostles." This manual originated sometime between the late first century and the early second century and contains directions for worship with a Christian congregation.[29] The instruction for baptism reads,

> Baptize as follows: after first explaining all these points
> . . . Baptize in the name of the Father and of the Son and
> of the Holy Spirit in running water. But if you have no run-
> ning water, baptize in other water; and if you cannot in cold,
> then in warm. But if you have neither, pour water on the
> head three times in the name of the Father and of the Son
> and of the Holy Spirit. Before the baptism, let the baptizer
> and the candidate for baptism fast, as well as any as are able.
> Require the candidate to fast one or two days previously.[30]

The "points" mentioned in the first line refer to preceding portions in the *Didache*, which read like a catechism for moral instruction, explaining how Christians are supposed to live. Once this has been explained and the candidates have understood, then baptism may be celebrated in the manner prescribed here.

Another of the early Christian sources comes from Justin Martyr, one of the church fathers, a teacher and defender of the Christian faith during a time of persecution. In his work *The*

Apology, dating back to 150, he writes the following instruction for baptism.

> Lest we be judged unfair in this exposition, we will not fail to explain how we consecrated ourselves to God when we were requested through Christ. Those who are convinced and believe what we say and teach is the truth, and pledge themselves to be able to live accordingly, are taught in prayer and fasting to ask God to forgive their past sins, while we pray and fast with them. Then we lead them to a place where there is water, and they are regenerated in the same manner in which we ourselves were regenerated. In the name of God, the Father and Lord of all, and of our savior Jesus Christ, and of the Holy Spirit, they then received the washing with water. . . . This washing is called illumination, since they who learn these things become illuminated intellectually.[31]

From both the *Didache* and the *Apology* we gain a glimpse of early baptismal practices.

Baptismal liturgies varied throughout the geographical regions of nascent Christianity; nevertheless, we find that three parts were practiced in common. First, candidates for baptism entered into a period of preparation and instruction.

Second, they submitted to a ritual washing. Third, they were blessed with the Trinitarian name. Let us look at each of these parts.

The baptismal process began with a period of preparation called the "catechumenate." In this time of instruction, the candidates learned about the faith they would soon profess and the community they were about to join. They studied the content of the faith and the practices of the Christians, namely, their rituals and the good work they performed in the care of the poor and the needy. They would listen to personal stories of those who had encountered Jesus or were transformed by their faith in Christ and by the life within the community. The length of time for this period is uncertain. Justin does not specify any length of time. We find mention of a three-year period of catechetical instruction in the document the *Apostolic Tradition*, written perhaps by Hippolytus of Rome around the year 217, "Let Catechumens spend three years as hearers of the word."[32] However, a subsequent document, the *Canons of Hippolytus*, which is derived from the *Apostolic Tradition* and dates back to the year 336, contains no reference to a three-year catechumenate. Instead, the community is instructed that "during forty days [the catechumens] are to hear the Word of God and if they are worthy they are to be baptized."[33] While we cannot determine a set duration of this period among the various early Christian communities, the early sources do make clear that there was a need for some time of instruction in the teaching and practice of the faith.

Let the catechumens become "hearers of the word," Hippolytus said. In other words, those who wish to become disciples of Christ must first listen to the Word of God and then respond by living a life of faithful obedience to his teaching. It is important to remember that the initiative for discipleship comes from God. In other words, God makes the first move. God speaks and we respond. All that we do in the name of God is but a response to God's grace, God's self-communication to us.[34]

During the period of the catechumenate, the candidates demonstrated their becoming "hearers of God's word" during the liturgy when they were dismissed from the congregation following the proclamation of the Scriptures and the preaching. They were dismissed so that they might further reflect on the word they had just heard and consider the influence it would have on their lives.[35] No doubt the dismissal of these individuals also served as a sign for those who remained inside the church—they too must continue to be hearers of the word.

The word *catechumen* is derived from a Greek word that refers to a person's undergoing a course of instruction. We find such references in the Letter to the Galatians, in which Paul writes, "Let him who is taught the word [*catechumenos*, literally "being instructed"] share all good things with him who teaches" (6:6 RSV).[36] The word also came to mean "reecho," in that the Christian community hoped to let their faith "reecho" in the candidate.[37] As the community engages in the process of the catechumenate, accompanying the candidates along the way, their own faith is "echoed" so that they may hear it again, perhaps in a new way. This echoing may be similar to a married couple attending a wedding ceremony. While they may have been married for many years already, in hearing the Scripture opened by the preaching and hearing the bride and groom pronounce the marital promises, they have an opportunity to reflect on their own marriage—not just remembering the wedding day but also reviving the meaning of their married life. The same could be said for a priest concelebrating a Mass of ordination: through the prayers offered for the one being ordained, the priest hears again his own commitment in response to God's promises. The newlyweds and newly ordained echo the promises made by the veterans of marriage and priesthood, recalling their own commitment of faith. Likewise, the catechumens provided an opportunity of renewal for the entire community as they listened and responded to the word of God.

One specific moment that demonstrated an echo of the faith occurred with the recitation of the creed. Those who were charged with guiding the candidates took great care to instruct them in the faith, which they then had to profess before being baptized. As a sign of their readiness for baptism, both the community and the candidates engaged in the *traditio et redditio symboli*, the "handing over and giving back of the creed." Those who were already baptized heard their own faith accepted and proclaimed by the new members.[38]

Having completed the catechumenate and proven themselves ready to be initiated into the community, the candidates underwent the rite of baptism itself. To imagine this baptism, recall Justin Martyr's description of how the candidates were brought to a "place where there is water" and there were washed. This washing, he explained, brings about a regeneration. They also referred to this washing as an "illumination" because the candidates would now be enlightened intellectually.[39] For Justin, baptism does not only cause the forgiveness of sins but also celebrates a new birth. Baptism celebrates the new life received through Jesus Christ and shared with the community of his followers. And like the Roman soldiers receiving the *sacramentum* with the seal of Rome by which they were recognized as members of the military, so too the neophytes are adopted by their community, who pledges its support of the individuals to follow the way of Christ. The persons have been reoriented, have changed the direction of their lives. They now walk with Christ in the company of his followers.

The washing itself, as mentioned earlier, followed the custom of either submersion or immersion. If the place of baptism stood by a deep pool of water, such as a lake or river, the person could be completely submerged and then raised up. If the pool of water were shallow, the person would either stand or kneel in the water, and the head would be pushed backward. Sometimes there was no source of running water, as mentioned in the *Didache*. In these cases, those baptizing used either the method of affusion (pouring water over the head of the person) or sometimes aspersion (sprinkling).[40]

These three parts of the early baptism ritual—the preparation of the catechumens, the washing as a sign of rebirth, and the invocation of the Trinitarian name of God—will probably sound familiar to you. But there is a fourth part that was also common practice for the early church but became separated from the ritual along the way. It is now less familiar. Returning to Justin's *Apology*, we read the following.

> After thus baptizing the one who has believed and given his assent, we escort him to the place where are assembled those whom we call brethren, to offer up sincere prayers for all other persons, wherever they may be. . . . At the conclusion of the prayers we greet one another with a kiss. Then, bread and chalice containing wine mixed with water are presented.[41]

We learn that the baptismal ritual included a celebration of the Eucharist.

As most celebrations, both sacred and secular, culminate with a meal, so did baptism. This fact meant that, for the new Christians—no longer catechumens—their union with the community was shown at the table of Communion, their first time to partake of the Lord's Supper. Of course, in the early church, people were baptized as adults with some exceptions for minors and infants. A short while later, when infant baptism became the standard, the washing was followed by the Eucharist with the infant receiving a drop of consecrated wine. Interestingly, this is still practiced among the Orthodox churches. Roman Catholics, however, discontinued this practice. During the eleventh century there developed in the church a growing reverence for the elements of the Eucharist. Indeed, the laity were no longer allowed to receive the cup of consecrated wine, Christ's blood, and hosts began to replace the loaves of bread. Because of this heightened reverence, a child's "first Communion" was postponed until the "age of reason," typically age seven or later.[42]

The Rise of Infant Baptism

The fact that those to be baptized gave their consent indicates that they were capable of making the decision for themselves to follow Christ. The personal testimony of freely given consent witnessed to a conversion in the person's life. This personal consent played an important part in baptism for the early church. However, by the second century, we know that infants were being baptized. Sources from the early church indicate that there was a good deal of discussion about this fairly new, infant baptism. Let us consider three sources from the third century.

Tertullian wrote in *On Baptism*, mentioned earlier, that he opposed infant baptism, which indicates that the practice must have been fairly common. He was concerned that baptism may be administered too hastily. While acknowledging that the Lord encouraged the little children to come to him, Tertullian advised, "Let them become Christians when they are able to know Christ. In what respect does the innocent period of life hasten to the remission of sins? . . . Let them learn to ask for salvation so that you may be seen to have given to him who asks." Tertullian emphasizes the need for one to ask for baptism so that a person can make a personal choice to conform one's life to Christ. Furthermore, his comment on sin reflects a concern of his time. This was the sin thought to be inherited through human nature, a stain attached to birth.

The Christian philosopher Origen then described the stain of sin this way. First he quotes the book of Job (14:4–5), "No man is clean of stain, not even if his life upon the earth had lasted but a single day." He then comments, "Through the mystery of baptism, the stains of birth are put aside. For this reason," according to Origen, "even the small children are baptized. For 'Unless born of water and the Spirit one cannot enter the Kingdom of Heaven'" (Jn. 3:5).

Origen expresses a growing concern of his day, the fear of dying while still stained by sin. And if one had not been baptized, one could not enjoy eternal life in union with God. As a result, the practice of "emergency baptisms" developed; that is, people young and old who were in danger of death would be baptized. Many burial inscriptions from this period claim, in order to testify to his or her salvation, that the person was baptized. For instance, one inscription for a young boy reads,

> Here lies the body of a boy to be named
> O blessed boy, the earth held you for a few days,
> An infant, and sent you back to the heavenly kingdom.
> You were born only so that you might attain to rebirth.

This switch in practice, we see in this inscription, was brought about because of the high rate of infant mortality and the concern that babies needed to be baptized within a few days of their births lest they die still stained with sin and not be reborn into eternal life.

Finally, in another third-century document, the *Apostolic Tradition*, mentioned above, we find this instruction: "And first baptize the small children. And each one who is able to speak for themselves, let them speak. But those not able to speak for themselves, let their parents or another one belonging to their family speak for them."[43]

The ritual for infant baptism followed, with slight modifications, the one for adults. For example, since infants could not respond to the questions of renouncing Satan and accepting Christ, godparents or ministers made the responses for them. This would have been expressed either in the third person, as in,

> Priest: "Does he renounce Satan?"
> Godparent: "He does renounce him."

Or in the first person:

> Priest: "Do you renounce Satan?"
> Godparent: "I do renounce him."

A philosopher of the fifth or sixth century, Pseudo-Dionysius, explains the role of the godparents this way.

> [The sponsor] does not say, "I am making the renunciations and the promises for the child," but "the child himself

is assigned and enrolled." In effect what is said is this: "I promise that when this child can understand sacred truth I shall educate him and shall raise him up by my teaching in such a way that he will renounce all temptations of the devil, that he will bind himself to the sacred promises and will bring them to fruit."

Some of the other ceremonies, naturally, were then discarded, such as the handing over of the creed and the reception of the Eucharist, while others remained, such as the prayer of exorcism, which prays that the newly baptized will be free from the tyranny of the devil, and the reception of the white garment, which displays the new person emerging from the baptismal bath.[44]

The switch from adult to infant baptism led to another ritual change for the Western church: the separation of the three sacraments of initiation (infant baptism, first Communion, and confirmation). In the Eastern churches it was common practice for a presbyter to administer all three sacraments on one occasion soon after the birth of a child. However, in some of the Western churches, it became the practice for a presbyter to administer baptism only to be followed by the first Communion several years later. Confirmation was then reserved to the bishop and conferred at a later date. This order of receiving the sacraments was changed in the eleventh century with the Eucharist being received last, due to the developing reverence for the sacramental species mentioned above.

Baptism and Table Fellowship

Here we might pause to consider if we have lost something along the way by dividing the one sacrament of Christian initiation into three separate sacraments: infant baptism, first Communion, and confirmation. Yes, perhaps we have. After all, early Christians always came to celebrate around the table of the Eucharist. In fact, before they were called Christians, the disciples of Jesus Christ were known as the people who broke bread together. They were true companions, according to the literal meaning of the word "companion," *cum pane*, "with bread." The communal breaking of the bread was, above all else, the true sign of Christian unity.

Moreover, Jesus invited many people to dine with him. These meals are never concerned with the food itself but with the message of salvation taught at the table. The Gospel of Luke may provide the best example of Jesus' table fellowship with the description of ten such meals. This was a true sign of union with Jesus. Recall when Jesus chose to eat with Zacchaeus, the tax collector, a man despised by many for his trade. Or when Jesus welcomed the woman who crashed a dinner party and washed his feet. We also remember the many references to the kingdom of heaven as a banquet where the faithful will be welcomed and feast abundantly and where they will enjoy eternal communion with the Lord. Also, in the Gospel of John, after the resurrection, Jesus appeared to his disciples on the beach and ate breakfast with them. We remember as well the two disciples on the way to Emmaus and how they were perplexed at the news of the "empty tomb," yet they instantly recognized Jesus in the breaking of the bread. Many Gospel stories clearly indicate that eating with Jesus brings one closer to God.

Accordingly, we baptize in order to bring people to the table to eat with Jesus, partaking of his body and blood. In light of this, we need to ask, is it wrong to exclude certain members of the community due to their age? If they receive baptism, should they not receive Communion as well? Some may protest, understandably, that the little ones are not ready to receive the Eucharist. But then we could also ask, since they are not capable of giving their consent, are they ready to be baptized? For a long while, the church has taught that a child may receive first Communion upon reaching "the age of reason." In this way one's first experience of receiving the Eucharist is celebrated as a "coming of age," a step toward maturity within the church. The marking of stages for the coming of age is important for a young person's development within a society—but this is not the purpose of the Eucharist. Have we transformed our Christian sacrament into something of a secular ritual, a social rite of passage?

We are baptized so that we may sit at the banquet table, joining the Son of God and the communion of saints in the meal of salvation. We may recall the message of Paul to the Galatians: "For through faith you are all children of God in Christ Jesus. For all of you who were baptized into Christ have clothed yourselves with Christ. There is neither Jew nor Greek, there is neither slave nor free person, there is not male and female, for you are all one in Christ Jesus" (3:26–28 NAB). Perhaps we could add, "There is neither young nor old."

Along with the Eucharist, the separation of confirmation presents a similar problem. We could ask, what does confirmation mean when separated from baptism? Some may answer that a young person has shown a readiness to accept the responsibility of living a Christian life, defending the faith and caring for the needy, thus proving a willingness to serve as a "soldier for Christ." These are noble sentiments, to be sure, but again we need to ask, is this the purpose of the sacrament? Specifically, just what are we "confirming" here in the salute to one's readiness for discipleship?

As shown earlier, early Christians thought of baptism as a soldier's pledge, the *sacramentum*. If we look to the feast of Pentecost as the model for receiving the Holy Spirit, we see that the apostles did not comport themselves as soldiers of Christ or as defenders of the faith. Rather, they acted more like cowards, crouched in fear, quietly celebrating their Jewish feast in that upper room in Jerusalem. And who would blame them, since they feared capture and persecution by the Roman authorities for being companions of Jesus. But then, unexpectedly, the Spirit of God broke in and enlivened them. Only after the Spirit enflamed his heart and loosened his tongue could Peter speak.

Now, one could make the argument that the delay of confirmation to the age of adolescence allows the church community to recognize how the Holy Spirit has been present in a young person's life, expressing gratitude for the divine assistance and praying for the person's continued fidelity. In this way the church "confirms" and celebrates the presence of the Holy Spirit in the life of this person. But again we ask, is this the purpose of the sacrament? We also run the risk of reducing confirmation to a parish commencement ceremony, as if it were a completion of study and service for the church, for which one is now entitled to a future Catholic wedding. Does such a delay of confirmation distort the sequence of call and response, as discussed earlier? In other words, God calls us and we respond. We never first make ourselves worthy to follow Christ. Rather, we are made worthy along the way of following Christ.

The poet George Herbert illustrates this notion, that we are made worthy by Christ, in his poem "Love Bade Me Welcome." Here the poet describes a scene in which God invites someone to a banquet, but the guest feels unworthy and hesitates to accept. However, the host convinces the guest that he has been made worthy already and that attending the banquet is an expression of gratitude.

Love bade me welcome

Yet my soul drew back

Guilty of dust and sin

But quick-ey'd Love, observing me grow slack

From my first entrance in,

Drew nearer to me, sweetly questioning,

If I lacked anything.

"A guest," I answer'd "Worthy to be here":

Love said, "You shall be he."

"I, the unkind, ungrateful? Ah, my dear

I cannot look on thee."

Love took my hand and smiling did reply,

"Who make the eyes but I?"

"Truth, Lord, but I have marr'd them; let my shame
Go where it doth deserve."
"And know you not," says Love, "who bore the blame?"
"My dear, then I will serve."
"You must sit down," says Love, "and taste my meat."
So I did sit and eat.

Herbert's poem reminds us that it is the Lord's call and our response in faith that renders us worthy.

Recently there has been some movement toward restoring this table fellowship. Clearly Roman Catholics are not ready to commune with young children before their "first Communion." However, in some dioceses around the country, the age for confirmation has been lowered. In some cases, children are confirmed before making their first Communion. But the greatest movement toward reuniting the three sacraments of initiation and restoring the table fellowship of Christians has come through the revised rite of baptism within the late twentieth century.

Revision to the Rite of Baptism

In the early 1960s, the Second Vatican Council met, having been convened by Pope John XXIII. It was a watershed moment for the Catholic Church as well as for many Protestant churches. The purpose of this council was to help the church to adapt to the modern world. The need for adaptation was especially strong in the area of the church's worship. The council fathers explained the need this way: "With the passage of time there have crept into the rites of sacraments and sacramentals certain features which have rendered their nature and purpose far from clear to the people of today. Hence some changes are necessary to adapt them to present-day needs."[45] With this concern in mind, the council called for the revision of the rites of worship.

The sacrament of baptism received the most extensive revision. The result was a new rite of baptism for children, which came into use in 1969, and a rite for adults, which began in 1972. This second rite was named "The Rite of Christian Initiation for Adults" and is usually referred to as RCIA. Now, up to this point we have referred to rites as celebrations that usually take place in church and that last about an hour. This rite, however, takes place over an extended period of time, from several months up to three years. This rite forges a path for a person of faith to follow Jesus Christ in a more profound way. Also, this path does not end with baptism alone but with the three sacraments of baptism, confirmation, and Eucharist.

The council addressed in detail the relationship of the three sacraments of initiation, and the result is a restored unity of the three sacraments. Today's *Catechism of the Catholic Church* clarifies this restored unity by referring to the "sacraments of initiation," citing the early church and its threefold practice of initiating adult converts through immersion, chrismation (anointing with oil), and participating at the table of the Eucharist.[46] Also, according to the *Catechism*, adult baptism is now considered the norm for the sacrament, in its preparation and reception, and infant baptism will be derived from this.

With the revision of the rites comes a shift in emphasis. First, while baptism does absolve a person from sin, we find now a greater emphasis on one's incorporation into the Christian community. Second, for confirmation, while the bishop is the ordinary minister of the sacrament, priests may administer the sacrament as well. Third, while the church maintains a hierarchy of roles within the community, there is a greater emphasis on the unity of a worshiping community, with the various roles cooperating within the body of Christ.

The RCIA is the primary pathway toward initiation into the Roman Catholic Church. Through this rite a community is formed, a band of seekers joined in the search for a closer relationship with the Lord. They are like the people who approached the disciple Philip, saying, "Sir, we would like to see Jesus" (Jn. 12:21 NAB). With their guides—their sponsors and catechists—they tread the path of the Christian tradition.

For those who have been seeking the Lord, having been called already by Christ, the rite helps them to express the object of their desire. Likewise, for the guides—those who testify for them and those who teach them—their faith is deepened by the probing questions of the seekers, forcing them to hear their familiar story in a new way. This pathway is laid out along a process of four "periods" punctuated with three "rites." Each of the periods marks a particular segment of the journey, and the rites celebrate the completion of a period.[47]

RCIA begins with a *quaestio*, that is to say, a question that places one on a quest or path of exploration and inquiry; it is a quest toward Christ. A person has become interested in the Catholic Church and feels called to learn more about the beliefs and practices of this community in order to discover if she should join. We will call this person a "seeker." At this point the only decision the seeker has made is to further her understanding of the church. This decision is probably the result of an invitation from the church's members who, in their own way, echo Jesus' words to his disciples, "Come and see" (Jn. 1:39 NAB). In embarking on such a quest, a seeker can only understand so much verbally and rationally. To truly experience the church, one must participate—by meeting its members, studying its beliefs, and engaging in its rituals.

When the seekers choose to continue their journey of faith, they then decide to enter the church, and they anticipate the day of their sacramental initiation. During this period, the catechumens learn to live as Catholic Christians. The philosopher Aristotle once noted that "the things we have to learn before we can do them, we learn by doing them."[48] Applying the philosopher's advice to the catechumenate, we could say that one learns how to be a Christian by acting as a Christian in concert with the community.

Church members accompany the seekers along the way. Each of the catechumens is assigned a "sponsor," who guides the catechumen in living out the gospel on a daily basis. They witness to the catechumen by offering themselves as models for Christian living. Later on they will also witness to the community for the catechumens, vouching that they are worthy to enter the church.

Catechumens attend the Sunday liturgy, participating in the Liturgy of the Word. They listen to the proclaimed Word of God and respond with the faithful in the responsorial psalm and the Gospel acclamation. After the homily the deacon or priest "dismisses" them formally, calling them forward and instructing them to leave the church with their sponsors and to meet as a group so that they may reflect on what they have just heard. They are sent off with the prayerful wishes of the church and with the anticipation of one day celebrating together fully with this community. The catechumenate marks a change in the status of the candidates. Although they are leaving now, they are joined to the church in which they are nourished by the Word of God and through the liturgical celebrations. They are joined to the extent that if they marry during this time they may follow the Catholic rite of marriage. And if they were to die, they would receive a Christian funeral and be buried in a Christian cemetery.

The journey culminates at the Easter Vigil, celebrated in the dark night of Holy Saturday, where the elect reach the final stage of their quest. The baptismal waters wash away their sins, and the anointing with chrism marks them as children of God. They are then brought to the table of the eternal banquet, where they may participate fully in the community's celebration and join their hopes with the Holy Spirit, who will lead them into the promised fullness of life. This is the "abundant life" promised by Jesus: "I came that they may have life and have it abundantly" (Jn. 10:10 RSV). During the Easter celebration, Christians renew their fidelity to Jesus Christ, who is Son of God and Savior of the world. They renew their hope in the resurrection and in everlasting life, believing that death shall not have the final word. The baptism of these candidates expresses this belief and hope in a vibrant manner. But the journey does not end here.

Baptism may be complete, but RCIA continues with the *mystagogia*. This ancient Greek term refers to the instruction for entering into a religious institution. It marks the moving forth of the whole community with the newly baptized as they continue to reflect on the Scripture, share in the Eucharist, and perform works of charity. Through the process of *mystagogia* the newly baptized will deepen their understanding of the paschal mystery, incorporating its practice in their daily lives.[49]

However, this whole process may be a case of easier said than done. The role of RCIA in baptism also leads to a possible challenge for the church. It is a recent phenomenon that a large number of those who complete the RCIA program leave the church shortly afterward, often within one or two years after their baptism. The problem seems to be that we have a great program for bringing people to the altar and initiating them into the sacraments. Along the way, these people are enlightened and supported by a company of ministers and a regular community. However, this support too often slips away after the water of baptism has dried. Likewise, the zeal of the convert may wane. Why? This may be due to disillusionment.

Perhaps a solution for saving these vocations is to follow the practice of some dioceses today and involve the new members immediately in parish activities. They may be recruited as liturgical ministers, catechists, or volunteers to those with special needs throughout the community. They should be invited to study sessions, spiritual retreats, and social gatherings. Baptism for adults does not mark the end of a lengthy process of initiation; rather, it begins a lifelong work of incorporation into the church, into the body of Christ.

In the ritual of baptism, a godparent lights a candle from the Easter candle and hands it to the newly baptized. The minister tells the baptized: "Walk always as a child of the light and keep the flame of faith alive in your heart." It is the responsibility of the church to tend this flame, supporting the newly baptized, helping them to maintain their faith.

the structure and symbols of baptism today

The best way to begin the study of theology is in church, with the celebration of ritual. Rituals tell the story of the sacraments and of the Christian faith in a succinct and expressive form. In the community's prayer and song, as well as in its symbols and gestures, we are introduced to the fundamentals of the faith. Here we learn by doing. The church's worship provides the primary setting for learning about our faith. If you want to learn about a religious group, then you should join them for worship.

The second place for learning about religious faith is the academy, or the classroom, where we reflect on and analyze what we have witnessed. Here we study the tradition of the church, exploring its history and doctrine, in ways suited to a contemporary understanding. In other words, we seek to make sense of and apply a tradition, one that is centuries old, to our current context of time and place. Theology is "done" in the church as well as in the classroom; that is, we learn our theology through the dual activities of worship and study.

As mentioned earlier, theology is the practice of "faith seeking understanding"; that is, theology begins with an act of faith, with a person's response to God's call. But in order to deepen one's relationship with God, one needs to reflect on this call and respond in the light of a rich tradition. This response shapes one's whole life, not just an hour on Sunday. Through the study of the tradition—the practical and the ethical—believers learn how to shape their lives, conforming themselves to the body of Christ. Greater understanding leads to a deepening of one's faith. So we can again say that theology begins in church.

Consider how the first followers of Jesus Christ kept the faith by meeting for worship to give thanks and praise to God. This was their initial response by which they dedicated Sunday as the "Lord's Day," a little Easter, commemorating the day on which Christ was raised from death. Eventually questions and problems arose concerning their faith. And as the original disciples passed away it became necessary to record and interpret their personal experience and understanding to future generations. This recording and interpreting took place especially with the spread of Christianity to other cultures, as believers faced the problem of translating the teaching into languages and cultures with different symbols and customs.

Perhaps the study of theology can be summed up with the question, asked within the context of ritual celebration, why do we do this? The Christian tradition unfolds from the regular practice of sacramental worship. The ritual of baptism begins this unfolding of the Christian story. Let us now look at this ritual in some detail.

There are five parts to the structure of a typical infant baptism. These are, first, the welcoming of the candidate along with family and friends to the church; second, the Liturgy of the Word, in which we hear the Scripture proclaimed and then a homily; third, the profession of faith, which is pronounced in dialogue with the minister asking questions and the people responding; fourth, the rite of baptism itself, which includes the water bath, an anointing with chrism, putting on a white garment, and receiving a candle; and fifth, the celebration concludes with a blessing.[50] The following is an example of how the ritual tells the Christian story.

Little Jennifer was brought to church one morning, her tiny body wriggling to break free. It was her first visit to church and the day of her baptism. She would be the third of my nieces I would baptize. The church was full for the usual Sunday

Eucharist, along with family and friends who traveled here for the special occasion. The full church was a good sign, a grand welcome for a new member and a show of support to the child's family.

Baptism is intended to be a communal celebration, and so it should take place when the community gathers for the Eucharist. If this is not possible, or deemed impractical, the relatives, friends, and neighbors are encouraged to participate, for they help to represent the community into which the child will be initiated.[51]

For this special occasion we began the liturgy by meeting at the entrance to the church. The congregation was asked to stand and to turn and face the entrance. The family, relatives, and invited friends gathered there, and I greeted them. In the name of the church, I ask the parents two questions: "What name do you give your child?" And they answered softly, "Jennifer." "What do you ask of God's church for Jennifer?" They replied, "Baptism." Following this ritual, I read a simple instruction to the parents, followed by a question to the godparents, "Are you ready to help these parents in their duty as a Christian mother and father?" They answered gladly, "We are."

Then I announced: "Jennifer, the Christian community welcomes you with great joy. In its name I claim you for Christ our Savior by the sign of the cross." I traced the marking of the cross on her forehead and invited the parents, godparents, and all others standing around the baby to do the same.

As the people pressed forward for the signing, I signaled the music director, and the church joined in singing the entrance hymn. The ministers, carrying candles and the Gospel book, led the family and their small entourage up the aisle, toward the sanctuary. The family filed into the first pews, and we continued our praise of God. The presence of young Jennifer today shows us that the church is growing still and that we continue to keep faithful to the Lord's command, teaching and baptizing in his name.

During the Liturgy of the Word, everyone participated as usual, perhaps on that occasion with a little more gusto. I like to think that the congregation spoke up for the little girl, who could not speak yet, but by their example they showed her how to participate. The reading of Scripture was followed by a homily in which the preacher opens the Word of God in order to relate this ancient story to the present occasion. This is the question behind all preaching: what is the Lord saying to us today through the sacred text? This is the ideal. Yet in answering this question, we should also be practical, and so, hopefully, the homily will be "short and sweet"—that is, brief but substantive. It should be brief. As I looked around, I couldn't help but notice that most of the congregation was looking toward the baby; she was of course stealing the show. Every movement and gurgle she made caught the attention of those around her. Also, the congregation was made up of many young families, friends, and peers of the parents with their own little ones. Some of these restless children had broken free from their pews and were roaming up and down the main aisle, exploring the church, their parents running to retrieve them.

This was not an occasion for a lengthy discourse on sacramental theology. I knew that. In looking around still, I noticed that we were joined by family friends from other faiths, some Jewish friends, a Hindu family, and also some Protestant friends of our family. Plus I saw some of my own relatives who left the Catholic Church long ago and now belong to that rising group of the "unaffiliated," who are not atheist but do not belong to any church. They consider themselves "spiritual but not religious." Standing at the pulpit, taking in this congregation, even the best of preachers would find this a challenge, trying to convey the Word of God to everyone!

We meet the same challenge at weddings and funerals. In celebrating these sacraments, the church doors are opened wide. Yet, with this diverse gathering comes an opportunity for catechesis, allowing those in attendance to hear the Word of God in a new way. We ask, what is the Lord saying to us—all of us—today in our celebration? Through all of these opportunities, we should always remember that sacraments are about more than the individuals involved. Jennifer's baptism was not solely about this little girl but about what God was doing for us in the here and now. So it is silly for the preacher to pretend to preach to the baby or to pander to the parents and guests about such a cute child. (This occurs at some weddings as well, when the preacher focuses on the couple and ignores the sacrament.) To be clear, the point here is not to command strict adherence to the rubrics of the ritual but that we should not lose sight of our purpose in the midst of the celebration. What is the purpose? Jennifer's parents and family had come to the church offering thanks for their newborn child, whom they considered to be a gift from God. The rather ordinary biological event of birth, in this instance, we consider a miracle, revealing the majesty and beauty of God. This miracle is certainly worth celebrating, which is why the homily should be short and sweet.

The homily at Jennifer's baptism lasted just five minutes. Afterward, we paused briefly before beginning the "Prayer of the Faithful." This prayer is the congregation's response to the Word of God we just heard proclaimed. I called the people to prayer, and Jennifer's older sister, a regular reader for the parish liturgy, read the petitions. They began with a prayer for

Jennifer herself and for all the recently baptized, then for her parents, and then the local community, followed by prayers for the entire church. The Prayer of the Faithful is called the priestly prayer of the people because here the faithful exercise their priesthood, the "priesthood of the laity." They intercede on behalf of all the people with whom they have contact and for whom they are concerned. This prayer is one specific instance of a response to the proclamation of God's Word.

From the earthly concerns of family and community, we lifted our eyes to the heavenly kingdom and prayed a brief litany of saints. I called out the names of several models of the Christian faith. Following the names of Mary and Joseph, the list included Saint Jennifer, Saints Barbara and Steven for her parents, and other appropriate names. After hearing each name, the people responded, "Pray for us." Hearing these names reminds us that we walk with many who have gone before us. We are part of a tradition that is centuries old. Through this prayer, we join with the communion of saints. Mementos of this august group surround us throughout the church building in painting, stained glass, and sculpture. "Today," I said, "we pray that Jennifer will carry on this long and rich spiritual tradition and walk with the saints."

The prayer of the people is followed by two brief prayers, an exorcism and an anointing. The first prayer need not conjure up the macabre images of a horror film. Rather, this prayer is a reminder of the reality of evil in the world and that we would be foolish to underestimate its power. So the church prayed that Sunday for the Holy Spirit to protect and preserve Jennifer—to seal her—against the influence of the evil spirit. Then she was anointed with the oil of catechumens. Recall how the ancient catechumens were supported by the whole community along the way to baptism. With this anointing, the child symbolically joined this order with the community's pledge of support.

Having completed all of this, I invited the family and the congregation to gather around the baptismal font. This parish did not have a permanent font, so a portable one was placed before the sanctuary. It looked like an ornate feeding trough or a small bathtub, large enough to hold an infant. The sacristan made sure to pour warm water into the font, and to do so as late as possible before the liturgy so it remained warm. This way Jennifer would not be shocked by cold water. With the parents standing so that they could face the congregation, I invited all of the children in the congregation to come and stand around the font. They rushed to the front, jostling for position. Some stared wide-eyed with anticipation. For many there, this was probably the highlight of the ritual, the moment they'd been waiting for.

When all were gathered, I rolled up the sleeve of my alb and dipped my hand into the water, raising it and letting the water drip back into the font. Then I blessed the water. Listening to the blessing reminds us of the dynamic images of water found throughout the Bible. In the prayers of blessing, we hear of the parting of the Red Sea, through which Israel escaped its slavery in Egypt. We recall the Jordan River, where Jesus was baptized by John. Throughout the Scripture, water has symbolized rebirth, a new beginning, a fresh start. We should keep in mind the polyvalent significance of water's symbolism, namely, that water is both productive and destructive. All earthly life relies on water. Humans, animals, and plants cannot survive without it. In this way water helps to produce life. But water can also be a powerfully destructive force: a tsunami brings waves of destruction to a coastal town; floods will ravage a low-lying plain, destroying lives and land. Water is a most powerful force of nature in both what it gives and what it takes away. The followers of Jesus had a great appreciation for water, as they relied on wells for daily survival and upon the sea for their livelihood; and they feared the sudden storm at sea, aware of its creative and destructive force. So, in the blessing of the water the minister acknowledges both of these forces, praying first to purify the one about to be baptized and then that through this water the person may die with Christ and be reborn with new life.

Having blessed the water, I turned to the parents and godparents and asked them to renew their own baptismal promises, reminding them of how they were to raise their child in faith. I invited the congregation to join in this prayer as well. As mentioned earlier, this renewal has two parts: a renunciation of sin and a profession of faith. The renewal is carried out in a dialogue format; the minister asks several questions concerning, first, their resolve to reject sin, and then their obedience to Christian teaching. To each of the questions, they respond, "I do." They figuratively move out of the darkness and into the light. They are drawn away from the evil spirit toward God's kingdom. This is what Jennifer's parents, godparents, priest, and entire community of faith vowed on her behalf.

I then signaled to the baby's mother and godmother, and they slipped her out of her onesie. Her older sister had forecast a smooth ceremony, noting that Jennifer likes to take a bath, so the full immersion, she thought, should work well. They handed her fragile, naked body to me. After baptizing my two other nieces in the same way, my sister trusted me with the care of her daughter! She had grown confident that I would not drop her accidentally. So I gripped her carefully, my left hand supporting her neck while the right hand held her legs, lifting her just above the water. Then I pronounced, "Jennifer, I baptize you in the name of the Father," and gently lowered her into the water up to her neck.

The children at the font watched with amazed looks. I continued the ritual, announcing, "And of the Son," accompanied by a second dunking, "And of the Holy Spirit," with a third dunking. Jennifer squirmed just a little, but overall she seemed to genuinely enjoy the bath, as her sister predicted.

I lifted the baby from the font. She looked around, seeming to take in the excitement around her. She was dripping wet, and I handed her to her mother and godmother, who carried her to a side table, dried her off, and dressed her in a small white gown, the same gown worn by her two older sisters at their baptisms. As we waited for the child, the congregation began to sing a Taizé chant. Its soft, repetitive verses are easy to follow without music sheets, and it has the effect of a lullaby, calming a baby.

When Jennifer was dressed, the women presented her for the anointing. At this point in the ritual, she received four symbols in quick succession. First, I applied the chrism to her forehead and prayed that she would remain forever a member of Christ, who is our Priest, Prophet, and King. In ancient times the anointing of a person showed that she or he held special status in the community. Kings and queens were anointed before taking the throne. In a similar respect, the baptized hold special status, as they are conformed to the body of Christ, sharing in his priesthood.

Then the parents wrapped Jennifer in a white garment, an "outward sign of Christian dignity" (no. 99). The color white is meant to signify purity. Often we see a tiny white bib placed on the child's chest, as if the seal of baptism were akin to a napkin protecting a person from food stains. Here too we should consider the fuller sign. Baptism is more about renewal than simply covering over an unsightly spot. So perhaps changing the clothing of an infant would better express this message. As we did in Jennifer's case, the baby could arrive in everyday clothes and then have them removed for the bath, and after dried off, she could be dressed in a white outfit.

For the third symbol, one member of the family carried a candle and lit it from the Easter candle. I then charged the parents and godparents to help the child walk in the light of Christ. The priest announces, "These children of yours have been enlightened by Christ. They are to walk always as children of the light." I remember saying these words solemnly, as I always do, but also with great feeling, as this was my own beloved niece. In the early church, the newly baptized were called the *illuminadi*, or the enlightened ones. Since an infant cannot be enlightened at this young age, it is the responsibility of those who care for her to see that someday she may truly wear this title.

The fourth symbol, called the *ephphetha*, or "prayer over the ears and mouth," is optional. The priest touches the ears and mouth of the child and says, "May the Lord soon touch your ears to receive his word, and your mouth to proclaim his faith." This symbol is reminiscent of Jesus' healing of a deaf man by touching his ear and saying "Ephphetha"—"Be opened" (see Mk. 7:33–34). Then, before the rite of baptism is officially over, we bless the parents. Within the context of the Eucharistic liturgy, I like to hold this blessing to the end, the usual place for the final blessing.

The church prays for the child's parents. I call the parents forward and ask them to face the congregation. I invite other friends and family and congregants to join me in this blessing. We first bless the mother: "May God bless the mother of this child. She now thanks God for her child. May she be one with her in thanking Him forever." We then bless the father: "May God bless the father of this child. With his wife, he will be the first teacher of his child. May he also be the best of teachers, bearing witness to the faith by what he says and does." Finally, the congregation is blessed: "In his goodness, may God continue to pour out his blessings upon all present." These final blessing prayers show how, in asking for God's blessing, we hope to express the pledge of the church to support this family in the care of their child. The idea that it takes a village to raise a child is nothing new in the Catholic Church!

The Cycle of Life: From Baptism to Death

On the day of his (her) baptism, N. put on Christ.

In the day of Christ's coming may he (she) be clothed with

glory. (from the "Rite of Funerals")[52]

As was the case with my beautiful niece Jennifer, the sacrament of baptism leads a person to the path of new life, both temporal and eternal. Baptism promises to assist the newly baptized in leading a life of holiness, protected from evil. Baptism also promises entry into the eternal kingdom of Jesus Christ.

We hear this reference to eternity, for example, in the prayers associated with the white garment: "See in this white garment the outward sign of your Christian dignity. With your family and friends to help you by word and example, bring that dignity unstained into the everlasting life of heaven" (no. 99). Also, when the godparents receive the candle, the minister says: "This child of yours . . . is to walk always as a child of the light. May he (she) keep the flame of faith alive in his (her) heart. When the Lord comes, may he (she) go out to meet him with all the saints in the heavenly kingdom" (no. 100). Baptism sets us on the proper path of our earthly life while pointing ahead to our everlasting life.

Much of the baptismal ritual, in fact, points to eternal life. Hopefully much later after baptism, when the time of our death comes, we are returned to the church, the same setting in which all of our baptismal promises took place. Then the congregation is reminded of the promises we made at that time—as well as the reward awaiting us in the next life. Always, the cycle of our lives moves us from birth and the rite of baptism through death and the funeral rite, to new life in the heavenly kingdom.

For this reason, the symbols displayed at our baptisms are brought back for us again at our funerals. First of all, as the coffin is carried into the church, the priest[53] sprinkles it with holy water and says, "I bless the body of N. with the holy water that recalls his (her) baptism of which St. Paul writes: 'All of us who were baptized into Christ Jesus were baptized into his death'" (no. 38). After the sprinkling, a white pall is placed over the coffin in remembrance of the garment worn at baptism. The prayer for this action is the one cited at the beginning of this section.

The priest uses incense at some point during the rite, for instance, during Mass, at the preparation of the gifts. It may also be used at the beginning or the end of the liturgy as well. Here the priest says, "With faith in Jesus Christ, we reverently bring the body of our brother (sister) to be buried in its human imperfection" (no. 46).

Throughout the funeral rite, great care and reverence is shown the body of the deceased, which mirrors the reverence shown to a person in baptism through the anointing with chrism, when the person is anointed as "priest, prophet, and king." The use of incense marks the church's action as especially reverent as we raise our eyes to the heavens and plead for the deceased: "to God who gives life to all things, that he will raise up this mortal body to the perfection and the company of the saints" (no. 46). As Saint Paul writes to the community at Corinth, "For we are the aroma of Christ to God among those who are being saved and among those who are perishing" (2 Cor. 2:15–16 RSV). Here Paul believes that ministers not only preach Jesus Christ, the wisdom of God, but they also manifest him.[54] This notion of the aroma of God evolved through early Christianity into a phenomenon called the "odor of sanctity," in which a scent signaled the presence of the Holy Spirit. Certain saints were thought to emit such an odor during their lifetime, and upon their death the scent was even stronger. Christians considered the odor of sanctity a mark of holiness. In contrast, moral corruption, they thought, reeked of the devil, emitting a strong stench of sulfur.[55]

Another symbol, found standing tall in the sanctuary, is the paschal candle, which is brought out especially for this occasion. The candle recalls the light received at baptism, a sign of enlightenment that helps to guide a person throughout the journey of life. Now the church prays, "Give him (her) eternal rest, O Lord, and may your light shine on him (her) forever." If ever there were a time to remember our past in the paschal mystery, it is at the hour of our death. For in this mystery we remember the passing over from adversity to triumph, from sorrow to joy, from despair to promise, from death to life. Like our Hebrew ancestors standing vigil in Egypt on the night of Passover, and then walking through the Red Sea to the Promised Land, Christians hope to pass over the limits of mortality—"to shuffle off this mortal coil"—and enter eternal life. The ancient Romans described a similar journey, in which the deceased was ferried across the River Styx to Hades, the eternal resting place. Before departing, two coins were placed on the eyes of the deceased, which would be used to pay the ferryman for his service. The Roman Catholic rite of *viaticum* resembles somewhat this Roman custom. *Viaticum* is the last Communion a person receives before dying. The word means "food for the journey," so the community sees to it that the dying person receives proper spiritual nourishment for the journey into eternal life.

Finally, while there are no godparents or sponsors for us at our funerals, the community as a whole serves this ministerial role. We do so in two ways: first, by accompanying the dying person through the final stages of life, and second, by consoling the family and friends of the dead. "It is this duty to strengthen the hope of those present and to foster their faith in the paschal mystery and the resurrection of the dead. In this way, the compassionate kindness of Mother Church, and the consolation of the faith, may lighten the burden of believers" (no. 17). This instruction—for the faithful to "accompany the dying person, along with the family and loved ones"—points to a vital responsibility in the Christian vocation, one that each of us must follow at some point in our lives. And at times, all those who are baptized in the name of Jesus Christ are called to accompany the members of the community.

We remember that when Jesus sent out his disciples, asking them to forgive sins and cure the sick, he sent them out "two by two." This way they could witness to the good work they accomplished and support each other along the way. We remember also the lesson of the last judgment, in which Jesus warns that those who care for the hungry, naked, sick, and imprisoned will enjoy eternal reward, while those who neglect them will be banished (Matt. 25:31–46). Is not this another way of accompanying one another, especially concerning those who are less fortunate and who are marginalized within society? The parable of the final judgment reminds the faithful that there will be an accounting of how well they accompanied one another in this earthly life.

And so, just as in baptism the community is called on to witness to and support the candidates for initiation into the church, so also at the other end of our earthly life. At baptism, the worshiping community, represented by the godparents or sponsors, is given explicit instructions on how they are to carry out their important role. In fact, these instructions apply to all Christians at all stages along life's way. We are all to serve as witnesses and to support everyone in the community whom we encounter. So then, when we reassemble for someone's funeral, we are able to resume our role of accompanying each other throughout this life to the next.

The Christian vocation entails the responsibility of witness and support: witnessing to the presence of Jesus Christ, who is realized through our own prayer and work, and supporting one another when challenged by temptation and despair. Celebrating, challenging, consoling—all play a part in this activity of accompanying, which is the mission of us all.

some current issues concerning baptism

We continue our discussion of baptism with a look at some current and controversial issues.

Such controversy necessarily plays a part in the task of theology. Inasmuch as theology is faith seeking understanding, for the moment we emphasize the verb "seeking." Faith is never stagnant; it strives for greater understanding, by which it grows and matures. Like the love of a happily married couple, their love for each other grows as they continue to learn about each other. Sometimes this happens in moments of challenge, or argument, or difference. The mystery of the other is never exhausted. So too with religious faith: certain questions will pose a challenge to one's faith, but this challenge may serve to expand one's knowledge of God and to deepen one's faith.

To be sure, theology by nature is somewhat fluid rather than solid. This is what it means to follow a "tradition." From the Latin word *tradere*, meaning "to hand over," tradition entails the handing over of beliefs, teaching, and customs from one generation to the next. In the process of handing over these cultural artifacts, some evolution occurs as we adapt the cultural wisdom to the current context. This does not mean that we change core beliefs and doctrine. Rather, the task of theology is to present these beliefs and doctrines in such a way that renders them pertinent to the current age. Following are five issues that pose a challenge to the traditional practice of baptism within the Roman Catholic Church. In each case, we hope that the controversy may lead to greater clarity.

How Should We Call God in Baptism?

We have seen that it is a long-standing tradition within the rite of baptism to pronounce the name of the Trinity: "in the name of the Father, and of the Son, and of the Holy Spirit." However, recently, some have called this "Trinitarian formula" into question. They find the constant use of the words "Father" and "Son" offensive because these are masculine terms and exclude the feminine. Their constant use may suggest that God is male and, as Mary Daly has opined, "If God is male then the male is

God."[56] Here we want to ask, what does it mean to be baptized "in the name of the Father, Son, and Holy Spirit"?

In the first place, the act of naming—being given or taking a name, or the bestowing of a title—is often part of an initiation, an act of being brought into a community. The naming of someone or something implies a relationship and connotes a sense of belonging. For example, one of the first acts for parents with their newborn child is to name the child, and they give the child their family name, a clear sign that this little one belongs with them. They form one family.

Second, if we look closely at the preposition *in*, we learn that this Trinitarian formula offers another instance of incorporation. To say, "I baptize you *in* the name of . . ." does not mean "by the authority of," as a policeman might command a civilian to "halt in the name of the law," or a messenger's delivering a proclamation "in the name of the king." Rather, if we examine the formula in its Greek origin, we find the word *eis*, meaning "into" instead of *en*, meaning "in." Technically speaking, by being baptized "into" the name of the triune God, one is baptized "into" the community of the Godhead. The Trinity exists as a community in relationship: the Father and Son are united and held in harmony by the Holy Spirit.

A problem for understanding the Trinity is that all too often we understand it in terms of three tenuously joined but separate entities. We hear, for instance, of the leaves of a shamrock or the layers of an onion, and how their separate parts are joined. However, at the heart of the Trinity is the unity of the Father and Son, with the Spirit acting as the unifying force. Perhaps we can take as an image of the Trinity the poetic phrase, "You cannot see the dancers for the dance." Two dancers move as one, kept in the flow by the music that engulfs them. Similarly, the Father and Son move as one, held together by the Holy Spirit. The community of the Trinity serves as a model for the human community in which the devotion to one another forms a lasting bond of unity. Baptism into the triune name is an invitation to join in a divine dance and to move with God.[57]

Those who raise the objection to the Trinitarian name raise a valid point. We should be wary of exclusive language that presumes the male gender whenever referring to God. While God is properly called "Father," there are numerous occasions when prophets and mystics refer to God as "mother." In short, God is much greater than any one image or title can comprehend. The use of inclusive language should help to expand our understanding of God. However, I would argue that the Trinitarian name for God when used in the rite of baptism presents a special case. Following are two reasons why this name should not be altered.

First, some of the proposed alternatives alter the meaning of this name. For instance, a short time ago it was quite common to hear a blessing "in the name of the Creator, the Redeemer, and the Sanctifier." This neutral formula served to eliminate the masculine and "sexist" titles for God. However, this formula presents a problem because it reduces the three persons to functions, ignoring the relationship within the Trinity. A person is a being-in-relationship. The Father and Son are persons vis-à-vis their relationship with each other. To change the name of the first person from Father to Creator would be like my introducing you to my father but calling him my "biological parent." While the scientific description is true, the title "father" means so much more. This is the problem with the functional language: each of the three persons is so much more than the function describes. In fact, looking at the alternative formula, we could say that each one creates, redeems, and sanctifies. Recall the passage from the beginning of the Gospel of John, which we cited in the introduction: "In the beginning was the Word, and the Word was with God, and the Word was God. . . . All things came to be through him, and without him nothing came to be. What came to be through him was life" (Jn. 1:1, 3–4 NAB). Through this "Word" all creation came into existence. And this Word, John goes on to explain, "became flesh and dwelt among us, full of grace and truth; we have beheld his glory, glory as of the only Son from the Father" (Jn. 1:14 RSV). The Son of God, then, shares in the act of creation.

Further, toward the end of this Gospel, in the section known as the Final Discourse, Jesus addresses his disciples one final time before his death, resurrection, and ascension. As he prepares to leave them, he promises, "I will ask the Father, and he will give you another Advocate to be with you always . . ." (Jn. 14:16, NAB). Jesus implies that he is the first advocate and that the Holy Spirit will replace him after he leaves them. We could say, lightheartedly, that we do not have a clear job description for the three persons of the Trinity. They appear to engage in multitasking, sharing their responsibilities. More to the point, a formula such as "Creator, Redeemer, Sanctifier" alters the meaning of the doctrine of the Trinity, reducing the persons to the functions and ignoring the divine relationship.

A second reason for preserving this name is that it is the name given to the first followers of Jesus, which the church has used throughout its history. This name stems from Jesus' command to his disciples, as we read from the conclusion of Matthew's Gospel. Now we must take care whenever we attempt to quote Jesus. Some may ask rightly, were these the actual words of Jesus, or could they be part of a baptismal formula that was in use at the time Matthew wrote his Gospel? While the question is valid, we should not overlook the fact that invoking the triune name became the practice of the early church. For example, as we saw in the discussion of the history of baptism, Justin Martyr provides an illustration of this practice. In his *Apology*, written in the second century, he gives instructions for baptism, emphasizing the use of water and invoking the Trinitarian name.

Baptism with water and the triune name plays an important role in Christian tradition because it provides a succinct summary of the Christian faith. The immersion in the baptismal pool symbolizes the faith in Jesus Christ, who died and rose again, through which we are freed from sin. The pronouncement of the three names professes faith in Jesus Christ as the Son of almighty God and Savior of humanity, whose presence is witnessed in the world today through the working of the Holy Spirit. This practice has been handed over from one generation to the next, which maintains the Christian tradition.

Where Is Limbo?

Will my baby go to heaven? This is one of the most painful questions I have heard asked when a baby dies before being baptized. It is one of the eternal questions: What happens to us when we die? Where do we go? Will we be together again in the afterlife? These questions loom large when we grieve over the death of an infant.

For a long time, Christians believed that a baby who died before baptism would not find its way to heaven but would reside for all eternity in "limbo." Today, as we address this issue, we must first ask, where is limbo? To answer such a question literally, according to tradition, we would say that limbo stands on the borders of heaven and hell. The name is derived from the Latin word *limbus*, meaning "edge" or "border." Christians once thought that limbo is a region on that eternal border, inhabited by the souls of unbaptized infants and of the righteous people who lived good and moral lives but died before the coming of Christ.[58]

However, we would search in vain for a description of this region in the *Catechism of the Catholic Church*. This is because the doctrine of limbo has never been an official teaching of the Catholic Church, surprising as that may seem. Furthermore, we find no mention of limbo either in Scripture or in the writings of the early fathers of the church.[59] Nevertheless, many Catholics seem familiar with the notion of limbo and are capable of explaining it as the abode for unbaptized babies. But if the church has never taught the reality of limbo, how did this story come about?

The discussion of limbo originally arose along with the development of the doctrine of original sin. Original sin describes the human condition into which we are born; that is to say, we humans are imperfect, we are subject to temptation, and we must struggle against being overwhelmed by evil. Baptism cleanses the person of the effects of this sin. Without this cleansing, one is excluded from the beatific vision and denied the enjoyment of eternal union with God. A passage from John's Gospel supports this position: "Unless one is born of water and the Spirit, he cannot enter the kingdom of God. That which is born of flesh is flesh, and that which is born of the Spirit is spirit" (Jn. 3:5–6 RSV). Here lies the crux of the debate about limbo: how may we reconcile the universal will of God for the salvation of the world with the necessity of baptism for individual salvation? In other words, is baptism absolutely essential for eternal salvation, or may one be saved without having received the sacrament?

Throughout its history, the church has had to contend with the sad reality of infant mortality and that many children die before having the opportunity to be baptized. And in the case of young children, they die in a state of innocence, having never committed sin. Since they were not yet of a mature age to rationally distinguish between good from evil, and to deliberately will to commit a sinful act, they cannot be held morally culpable. In short, a young child cannot commit sin. Nevertheless, while one may not be capable of committing a sinful act, the stain of original sin blots the souls of the newborn and aged alike. Because of this sin, many Christians thought that, without baptism, one was barred from the kingdom of God and from eternal salvation.

The question, then, which was debated for centuries, focused on where, or how, one exists throughout eternity, having died without the benefit of baptism. Through the Middle Ages, and even up to the twentieth century, theologians believed that unbaptized deceased infants, although innocent, would suffer some form of torment. Some theologians held that they would suffer the pain of loss, being separated from God, and that this may be a blissful state in which they are not aware of the joy of which they are deprived. These souls were transferred to a special place, or state of being, named "limbo." Others held that the deceased would suffer a "pain of sense," enduring the fires of hell alongside the unrepentant sinners.

The issue of limbo emerged in a fierce debate in the late eighteenth century, beginning at the Synod of Pistoia in 1786. There, a group of theologians called the Jansenists attacked the notion, arguing that limbo was a fable invented by Pelagius, a philosopher of the fourth century, and developed later by the Scholastics during the Middle Ages. They claimed that their teaching, a rather harsh-sounding doctrine which claimed that unbaptized infants were doomed to hell, was indeed revealed doctrine, and they denounced the proponents of limbo as heretics. Several years later, in 1794, Pope Pius VI responded to the Jansenists in his bull *Auctorem Fidei*.[60] This bull is the only official document containing the word *limbo*. The bull does not argue for the existence of limbo but defends the church's teaching concerning the plight of the unbaptized. As a result, the rigid teaching of the Jansenists was dispelled, and theologians no longer argued that infants who die without baptism were sent to hell.[61]

Recently the discussion of limbo has been revived, due in part to the growing number of unbaptized infants who have died. This number includes the multitude who have been lost to abortion. Moreover, today many people find it difficult to accept a just and merciful God who excludes infants from eternal happiness while they have no personal sin. Consequently speculation about the salvation of these infants has taken on renewed significance. In 2007, the International Theological Commission (ITC), in its study "The Hope of Salvation for Infants Who Die Without Being Baptized,"[62] argued strongly for the salvation of the innocent. This study was approved by Pope Benedict XVI. The argument by the ITC for the salvation of unbaptized infants may be summarized according to three points, which follow the tradition of the church. This is to say that we find the foundation for this argument in the prayers of the liturgy and throughout selected passages from Scripture, as well as with the recognition that there are other means of baptism than with water.

The liturgical principle *lex orandi, lex credendi* says that the faith of the church is founded on the prayer of the church. Recall that earlier we explained that theology begins in church with worship. The liturgy is an authority—a foundation—for what we believe as Christians. So it is important to note that there is simply no mention of limbo anywhere within the church's liturgy. For instance, at no point throughout the entire liturgical year do we pray for the souls in limbo. Yet we do pray for the souls of those who died without baptism. Consider the Feast of the Holy Innocents, celebrated on December 28. The concluding prayer of this festal liturgy reads, "Lord, by a wordless profession of faith in your Son, the innocents were crowned with life at his birth. May all people who receive your holy gifts today, come to share in the fullness of your salvation." The ITC explains that these innocents are venerated as martyrs even though they were never baptized.[63]

Another liturgical consideration is the funeral rite for children. The instruction for the rite notes that in the case of a child whom the parents intended to baptize, yet who died prematurely, the bishop may allow a regular funeral to be celebrated for the child.[64] The church recognizes that while baptism is important for personal salvation, the infant has not placed any obstacle in the way of redemptive grace,[65] implying that the church recognizes the innocence of the child and acknowledges the intention of the parents. We might hear the following prayer read aloud at such a funeral: "Lord, listen to the prayers of this family that has faith in you. In their sorrow at the death of this child, may they find hope in your infinite mercy."[66] The mention of God's "infinite mercy" here is significant because God's mercy trumps all human endeavor. We should not underestimate the abundant mercy of God. We are reminded of this in another prayer, one with the sober title "Blessing of Parents after a Miscarriage." It reads, "Father and Creator, in whom all life and death find meaning, we bless you at all times, especially when we have need of your consolation. (These parents) *entrust to your care a life conceived in love.* May your blessing come upon them now. Remove all anxiety from their minds and strengthen this love so that they may have peace in their hearts and home. . . . Amen."[67] These prayers invoke trust in God's mercy for the care of the child.

The second point in the argument for the salvation of the innocent comes from a review of the New Testament. As stated earlier, the passage from the Gospel of John (3:5–6) helped to create this conundrum with the claim that without a rebirth in water and the Holy Spirit a person cannot enter the kingdom of God. However, we also find occasions in Scripture when the faith of some people may bring about the salvation of others. The ITC cites a passage from the Gospel of Mark (2:1–12 RSV) in which four men carry a paralyzed man to Jesus. In this scene, Jesus is at a home, and a crowd has gathered around him, pressing on him and preventing the men from entering the house; so they scale the roof, cut an opening in the tiles, and lower the man down to Jesus. The Evangelist Mark records that "when Jesus saw their faith he said to the paralytic, 'My son, your sins are forgiven.'" The ITC comments that while the normal way to salvation is through baptism in itself, the church hopes that there may be other ways to achieve the same end. Perhaps the principle to remember here is stated by Saint Paul: God "desires all men to be saved" (1 Tim. 2:4 RSV).[68]

These observations lead us to inquire if, indeed, sacramental baptism is necessary for salvation. With some precision, the ITC responds that sacramental baptism is a necessity but not an absolute necessity for salvation. It is necessary as "the ordinary way established by Jesus Christ to configure human beings to himself."[69] Nevertheless, the church has never taught the absolute necessity of baptism but allows for other avenues whereby this configuration with Christ can be realized. For example, the early Christian community accepted that a "baptism of blood" by a martyr was a suitable substitute for baptism with water. In this case, a person may have been preparing for baptism but during the time of preparation had been arrested with a group of Christians and suffered the same fate as they did. This person was recognized and respected as a martyr along with the baptized Christians. Furthermore, the church has long accepted the notion of "baptism by desire," in which a person who truly desired baptism but was not able to receive the sacrament could obtain salvation, as stated by the Council of Trent: "After the promulgation of the gospel, this transition (from sin to justice) cannot take place without the bath of regeneration *or* the desire for it."[70] Thus, on the one hand, one who wishes to be united with God through Jesus Christ cannot be opposed to sacramental baptism, for this is the ordinary way by which one is configured to Christ, and Christ commanded it to his apostles. On the other hand, the power and freedom of almighty God may not be limited by the sacraments of the church.

We might try to look at the question from God's point of view, if we may be so bold. The argument for limbo seems to emanate from a need to present the unbaptized infant to God through a carefully devised legal system. In this case, the church authority acts as the advocate of the deceased, justifying the person's claim to an eternal peaceful rest through the proper ecclesiastical procedures. The church authority therefore remains true to its teaching. However, we may imagine looking at the deceased from the divine judgment seat on which sits the Lord God, who creates out of nothing and for whom nothing is impossible.

In the words of the ITC, "God's power is not restricted to the sacraments. God did not bind his power to the sacraments so as to be unable to bestow the sacramental effect without conferring the sacrament. God can therefore bestow the grace of baptism without the sacrament being conferred (especially) . . . when the conferring of baptism would be impossible."[71] Here is one instance in which the church professes its reliance upon the mercy of God. We recall the plea of Jesus to his disciples, "Let the children come to me, do not hinder them" (Mk. 10:14), and trust that there is indeed a way of salvation for the children who die without baptism.[72]

Can One Undo the Indelible?

The Christian sacrament of baptism proudly proclaims that a person is marked for life as a member of the community that bears the name of its founder, Jesus Christ. And, like the *christos*, the "anointed one," all who are baptized are anointed with the threefold role of priest, prophet, and king. To state it simply, through baptism we know who we are and whose we are: we are sons or daughters of God, and we belong to the community called church. It is reassuring to know that once baptized, nothing can separate us from the love of God (Rom. 8:38–39).

Recently, however, this reassurance has been called into question. A movement that began in Great Britain, and has washed up on the shores of America, and has stretched across the Pacific to Australia, celebrates a ceremony called "de-baptism."

For example, on Sunday, October 26, 2008, a gathering of atheists celebrated de-baptism at the Texas Freethought Convention in Austin, Texas. The group leaders, dressed simply in T-shirts and jeans, made the pronouncement over the members: "In the name of secularism, in the name of reason and science, I de-baptize you." As the rest of the group responded with laughter and yelps of approval, the members individually stepped forward and allowed the leader to wave a handheld blow-dryer over them, signifying a drying up of the waters of baptism. Each member then received a certificate of de-baptism explaining that they have been "properly, and with due consent, de-baptized away from all religion into a more sane experience."[73] The leaders then proclaimed, "You are reason-based. You are rational." And the members responded, "We make sense. We sleep in on Sundays."[74]

Far away, on a beach in Queensland, Australia, we find another group presided over by "Pope Alice." This syncretistic group employs symbols from many of the world's religions as well as promoting belief in extraterrestialism. They proudly espouse apostasy in order to renounce the "war, genocide, and massacres committed in the name of God."[75] They intend to disassociate themselves from their churches and live as secular humanists. To demonstrate their new status, they walk down the shore into the ocean, submerging themselves, purifying themselves with no help from a church minister.

One "certificate of de-baptism" reads as follows.

I, _____, having been subjected to the Rite of Christian Baptism in infancy (before reaching the age of consent), hereby publicly revoke any implications of that Rite and renounce the Church that carried it out. In the name of human reason, I reject all its Creeds and other such superstition in particular the perfidious belief that any baby needs to be cleansed by Baptism of alleged ORIGINAL SIN, and the evil power of supposed demons. I wish to be excluded henceforth from enhanced claims of church membership numbers based on past baptismal statistics used, for example, for the purpose of securing legislative privilege.[76]

Performing a mock ceremony, a cultlike group gathers in a public setting and engages in a symbolic drying up of the baptismal water. The group members wish to register their protest against their religion and their desire to rescind their membership. No ecclesial authority, however, can force anyone to remain in the church; one is free to leave at any time. We may wonder why they do not simply walk away. It is as if they reject the option to go quietly into that dark night but choose to rage against the darkness of religious deception, as they perceive it.

In viewing and listening to the ceremonies, there seems to be a felt desire to express the breaking of the bond of baptism. In most cases these protestors were baptized as infants and so could not enter freely into the promise of the sacrament. They claim that religion was imposed upon them. Also, in some cases, they wish to symbolize the end of a relationship, anticipating a new stage in their lives; something new, however vague, is happening. For a sacramental theologian, priest, and teacher (like me), all of the protests and mock ceremonies raise some important questions: Can we undo the indelible? Can the mark of baptism be erased? Or, if this *sacramentum* is indeed permanent, is one free to leave the fold, not just physically but existentially, denouncing Christianity, its teaching and practice?

Perhaps we could make a comparison with another situation of separation: the renunciation of one's homeland. This situation entails the dissolution of a relationship through a legal process without benefit of a ceremony; the persons involved virtually walk away from their previous bonds in hopes of beginning a new stage in their lives. Renouncing one's homeland entails more than finding employment, or a pleasant climate, in a foreign land. One leaves home protesting an offensive national policy. For example, recall the African Americans who chose to leave the United States of America because of the pain of racial discrimination. They sailed to the shores of Africa to found the nation of Liberia. Their leaving, a public renunciation of their national heritage, signaled a protest against America. The proponents of de-baptism find themselves in a somewhat similar situation. However, if national defectors can move to another land where they may register for new citizenship, then where can the former Christians go? How will they express their new identity? And even though some may choose to leave their homeland, the national and ethnic roots cannot be removed so readily.

The phenomenon of de-baptism recently became a legal issue when one man sought to have his baptismal record removed from the parish registry. John Hunt, a medical doctor, fifty years old, was baptized into the Church of England as an infant, but during adolescence he drifted away from the church. In 2007, he learned of a Spanish court ruling that allowed Catholics to renounce their faith, and he sought to do the same. He petitioned the Church of England to have his name removed from its registry. The church refused to do so, explaining that the records are kept for historical purposes and they do not bind anyone to the institutional church. The church, however, did compromise by making a notation next to his name in the registry. In the Spanish case, the Supreme Court of Spain ruled that, since baptismal books are not record books but a "pure accumulation" of information, they are not subject to government rules.[77]

Hunt's protest sparked a movement, and soon thousands more requested a formal dismissal. Britain's National Secular Society (NSS), originally founded in 1866, created a certificate of de-baptism, which can be obtained from its website.[78] By April, 2009, more than one hundred thousand certificates had been downloaded.[79] However, the NSS is not the sole provider of these certificates. Across the English Channel, the Italian Union of Rationalists and Agnostics (UAAR) has distributed electronically more than sixty thousand within the last five years.[80] Raffaelo Carcano, the UAAR site manager, comments: "We see a traffic spike every time the Pope says something unpopular."[81] Across the Atlantic, in Argentina, a secularist movement, Collective Apostasy, supports bloggers with their notices concerning de-baptism.[82]

At the core of this conundrum is the practice of infant baptism and the claim by some that they were baptized unwillingly. Thus the mock ceremony of either blow-drying or rewashing appears to be an attempt to reclaim personal sovereignty and independence from an institution whose beliefs and values they never personally accepted; if anything, they were foisted upon the innocent. De-baptism, then, focuses on the symbolic separation from Christianity.

There does exist a more legal and sober approach for the disaffected. They may apply for the status of "defectors." "Defection" is a legal process by which one abandons the church community. Within the Roman Catholic Church, this process is referred to as *Actus Formalis Defectionis ab Ecclesia Catholica* ("formal act of defecting from the Catholic Church"). The process is found in the *Code of Canon Law* (specifically canons 1086–811, 1117, and 1124) and pertains to the sacrament of marriage. A commentary on these canons explains that the concept of "defection by a formal act" is an innovation of the recent code, and its exact meaning has yet to be determined.[83] Nevertheless, we learn that a "formal act" may consist of making a public declaration of abandoning the Catholic faith, either in writing or orally before two witnesses. Also, if one formally enrolls "by some external sign" in another church or religion, the church may consider this a formal act. A crucial component for this formality is the person's intention, namely, one must deliberately intend to leave the church. Without such intention, one's defection is in question. For example, in countries that impose a church tax, if one claims to defect simply to avoid paying this tax, the primary intention may be for relief from a financial burden rather than because of a disagreement with the church. Similarly, if a person announces a defection for the sake of appeasing a fiancé or future in-laws, the intention is also questionable.[84]

A recent document, or "notification," published in 2006 by the Pontifical Council for Legislative Texts, has helped to clarify the process. The notification was approved by Pope Benedict XVI.[85] According to this council, defection indicates "a true separation from the constitutive elements of the life of the Church: it supposes . . . an act of apostasy, heresy or schism." Defection also implies a rupture of the bonds of communion, faith, sacraments, and pastoral governance—from which the faithful draw the life of grace within the church.[86]

There are three requirements for the valid conferral of a defection. First, a person must make a decision to leave the church. The decision must be personal and given sufficient reflection. Second, the person must manifest this decision to family members and to a competent ecclesiastical authority. Third, this authority must receive the decision.[87] It is interesting to note that the person requesting defection does not need to offer a reason for the request. When a person has formally defected from the church, this should be noted in the baptismal registry.[88]

A formal "declaration of defection from the Roman Catholic Church" reads as follows.

I, _____, do hereby give formal notice of my defection from the Roman Catholic Church. I want it to be known that I no longer wish to be regarded as a member of the Roman Catholic Church. I further declare that I am aware of the consequences of this act regarding the reception of the sacraments of the church, including the sacraments of the Eucharist, marriage and the sick, and also with regard to burial. I undertake to make this decision known to my next of kin and to ensure that they are aware of these circumstances in the case of my being incapacitated. I acknowledge that I make this declaration under solemn oath, being of sound mind and body, and in the presence of a witness who can testify as to the validity of this document.

An unfortunate thing, and yet, the Catholic Church has created a reasonable avenue by which one may effectively and officially leave the church. And yet, take note: The Pontifical Council explains that defection is not to be considered a de-baptism.

We read: "It remains clear, in any event, that the sacramental bond of belonging to the Body of Christ, conferred by the baptismal character, is an ontological and permanent bond which is not lost by reason of any act of fact or defection."[89]Again, we could simply pose the question, why not just stop going to Mass, and leave quietly? However, for these defectors it is a matter of principle, and so there is a felt need to make a personal, symbolic statement.

How should the ministers, parents, and leaders in the churches respond? What should we do? I suggest three things. First, experience teaches us that disagreement can create an opportunity for dialogue. Some are confused about the teaching of the church. It would help for them to meet with a "wise elder," that is, one who is capable of explaining the principles of the church. Second, far too many people, both Catholic and non-Catholic, perceive the church as a monolithic institution whose members blindly follow the dictates of the pope. While Catholics are indeed obedient to the pope, the church is a huge body, which has developed through two millennia and stretches across the globe. This body is capable of embracing a multitude of cultures and ideologies, welcoming conservatives and progressives, high church and low church, the devout and the doubter. All are welcome here. Third, we realize that, even though some may leave the church, we do not believe God has left them. On the contrary, we trust in the mercy of God to accompany them along their way. And the minister should make clear that the church door remains open to them.

Although one is free to leave, it is futile to argue for undoing the indelible, for the rebirth of baptism into the Christian community is similar to entering one's family of birth. While one may denounce one's family of origin, or disown a family member, one cannot deny one's heritage and the rootedness in a particular human family. Of course the church cannot deny anyone the right to leave its ranks, which would be the equivalent of erecting a virtual Berlin Wall, turning the community into a compound. However, neither can the church rescind its promise offered in the pledge of baptism. Recall the prayer of anointing: "He now anoints you with the chrism of salvation, so that, united with his people, you may remain for ever a member of Christ who is Priest, Prophet, and King."

The seal of baptism cannot be undone because within the ritual of the sacrament the church acts in the name of God. The church acts *for* God. The church acts *as* God does in relation to human beings. The indelible bond of baptism cannot be undone; this undoing would contradict a fundamental belief of Christianity, namely, that God cannot and will not turn away from any person. The bond cannot be broken by God. The conundrum of de-baptism should lead scholars of sacramental theology, and all Christians, to a deeper understanding and appreciation of the indelible character of baptism.

Who May Baptize?

The proper minister of the sacrament is a deacon, priest, or bishop of the diocese in which the baptism is celebrated. Within his own diocese a priest or deacon may presume permission to baptize, but when traveling to another diocese, they will seek permission from the bishop of that diocese. Before traveling to baptize my niece Jennifer, I formally asked for permission from the pastor of her parish, and he in turn secured permission with his bishop. So the ordinary minister is one who is ordained.

However, the church allows for a person who is not ordained to administer the sacrament in the case of an emergency. Indeed—this may surprise you—even a non-Catholic may do so. Specifically the church instructs us as follows: "In imminent danger of death . . . when no priest or deacon is available, any member of the faithful, indeed anyone with the right intention, may and sometimes must administer baptism." This is nothing new. In 1439, the Council of Florence decreed that while the minister of the sacrament is the priest, "in case of necessity, not only priests or deacons, but also laymen or laywomen, or even pagans and heretics may baptize, provided they observe the Church's form and intend to do what the Church does."[90]

The church encourages all laypersons to participate as an exercise of a "priestly people." These laypersons include first and foremost the parents, as well as catechists, midwives, social workers, nurses, physicians, and surgeons. It is recommended that they be aware of the proper method of baptizing in the case of an emergency.[91] It is one more example of how the church, serving as the Body of Christ, extends the reach of the Lord to his people.

Should We Baptize Babies?

Most likely, American Catholics have witnessed more baptisms of infants than of adults. For Catholics, it is a fairly common celebration. So it might strike some as a strange question, whether we should baptize babies. However, this question has stirred up controversy throughout the church's history, and still does today.

Earlier in the book, we saw that this question has roots in the third century. While some were concerned with removing the stain of original sin, others cautioned against rushing into baptism without the opportunity for a personal profession of faith. Indeed, we saw that infant baptism emerged as "emergency baptism" in order to prevent an innocent child from dying with the stain of sin and losing the chance for eternal rest with God. Eventually infant baptism became the norm for Christianity, extending through the Middle Ages and up to the Reformation. Some of the Protestant Reformers then challenged the practice. They called for "believer's baptism," which required a personal confession from one who claimed to follow Jesus Christ, and they said that baptism should be the result of conversion. They found the roots for this personal confession in the New Testament, where men and women came forth to be baptized, stating their personal desire to follow the Lord.

The crux of the issue is whether we should baptize someone who is incapable of professing faith. All along we have discussed the sacraments in terms of a dialogue between God and a person of faith, indicating that God calls and the person responds. Obviously the infant cannot respond. So would it be better, for the sake of a meaningful celebration of the sacrament, to postpone the baptism until the person reaches a mature age and is capable of offering a faith-filled response? Otherwise it could appear that we baptize for a "negative reason," that is, for the removal of original sin, rather than for the "positive reason" of joining the body of Christ.

This issues of one's personal profession of faith raises a second concern for infant baptism. If the person is joining this community, he or she must be accompanied in the journey of faith. And this responsibility to accompany the person presents a problem. It is no secret that baptism is occasionally reduced to a cultural event, a social celebration lacking any spiritual significance. Sometimes there is a question about the ability of the parents to raise the child in the faith. Some parents may not be ready for this; others are really not interested in the life of the church. This situation is a problem today especially given how challenging it can be to live as a faithful Christian in our culture.

Not too long ago, the parish church constituted the center of a neighborhood. For Catholics the church was a gathering place. I remember, growing up in Brooklyn, New York, my friends and I were at the church seven days a week—and twice on Saturday. On Sunday we attended the children's Mass at nine in the morning. From Monday to Friday we attended the parochial school, which stood adjacent to the church. Then on Saturday morning in the springtime, we met there again and headed off to play baseball with the CYO (Catholic Youth Organization). After the game we returned to the church and went inside, where we stood in line for confession. Also, throughout the year, the church was central to our daily lives. We ate fish on Fridays and fasted before Communion. We wore ashes for Ash Wednesday, carried palms on Palm Sunday, and dressed up for Easter. The regular contact with priests and nuns, along with our friends and their parents, helped to form young Catholics in their faith.

Times have changed, and our formative religious environments have given way to a pluralistic society, a melting pot of cultures and creeds. The social support has diminished, placing greater responsibility on the parents and pastor to see that a child will be raised properly in a life of Christian faith. How difficult it is to raise a child in the church today. Would it not be more meaningful to wait until the child is capable of making a personal decision?

However, I suggest that there may be another way to look at this issue. Because it is so difficult to raise a child, not only in the church but also in society at large, maybe this is reason for baptizing infants. Indeed, the diminishment of the Christian subculture may heighten the responsibility of the community who is receiving the child. It takes a parish community to raise a Christian child.

One problem with the argument against infant baptism is that it focuses on the individual's faith and suggests that one comes to faith on one's own.[92] Now, while it is true that, in the dialogue of faith, God calls and a person responds, nevertheless in order for a person to respond to God, a community is necessary. The community makes it possible for a person to hear the call and respond to it. The call and response of faith occurs within the context of a Christian story. We must know the story in order to recognize the voice of the Lord and to interpret its meaning for us and to learn how to express our response.

This triune relationship of God-individual-community is illustrated by the story of the call of Samuel (1 Sam. 3:1–9 RSV). Samuel is a boy just twelve years old, the same age as Jesus when he was found in the temple talking with the rabbis. It is night and Samuel is asleep, but he is awakened when he hears someone call him by name. He replies, "Here I am." He thinks it is Eli calling him from the next room, so he runs to him. Eli is a wise, old man. But Eli tells him that he did not call and sends him back to bed. This happens again and again. After the third time Samuel runs to Eli, the old man realizes that it is the Lord calling to Samuel, so he tells the boy, "Go, lie down; and if he calls you, you shall say, 'Speak, LORD, for your servant hears.'" Samuel does as he is told, and the Lord calls to him again. Samuel answers as Eli instructed, and the Lord makes him a great prophet to Israel. Because of Eli, Samuel learns who is calling him and how to respond to the call.

I think of Eli as the church, a wise elder who knows the Christian tradition and who can speak for God. Meanwhile, Samuel represents the young child who is called by God to a life of faith. Eli provides young Samuel with the ability to recognize the call of the Lord and the language with which he may express his desire to follow the Lord. In his confusion over the Lord's visit to him, two questions arise: What does this mean? and, What do I say? How does one answer these questions except by relying on the wisdom and support of the community? The story of Samuel shows us that, for infant baptism to remain a viable practice for Roman Catholics, the church community must play its part. The Catholic subculture may have diminished, but the members of the community must assume their role in guiding the faith of the younger members through education, worship, and living the faith daily.

But what about sin? Our focus on the role of the community in infant baptism does not ignore the effects of sin on human beings. In fact, an understanding of the person as a social being will sharpen our view of original sin. This sin is better understood in terms of our relationships with other people rather than as a stain on a solitary soul. Earlier we defined "sin" as a distraction from following what we know is good. And we defined "original sin" as the human tendency toward evil. While human beings are essentially good, having been made in the image and likeness of God, we are not perfect, so we are given to distraction and suffer the effects of temptation. When the church accepts children into the fold, it pledges to guide them to live in right relationship with other people and with God, steering them toward virtue and away from vice. Baptism acknowledges the power of sin over an individual but reverses its influence through the grace of Jesus Christ and the guidance of the church.

The human being is essentially social and is not meant to live in isolation. One becomes a person by living in relationship with other persons. The family and the community help a child to develop into a person. For this reason the family is considered a "domestic church." We find this description in the document *Lumen Gentium* ("the light of all nations,"), or "The Dogmatic Constitution on the Church," from the Second Vatican Council. In it we read, "In what might be regarded as the domestic Church, the parents, by word and example, are the first heralds of the faith with regard to their children. They must foster the vocation which is proper to each child." The church sees the child's potential as a person of faith. This potential of faith means that, from the viewpoint of the church, it is not the case that the infant has no faith yet. Rather, the child's faith lies dormant, waiting to be exercised. What an important distinction!

Thomas Aquinas compared the infant's faith to a sleeping adult. We may presume that the adult is a virtuous person but while sleeping is incapable of acting virtuously. Likewise, the infant is not yet capable of acting like a person of faith but has the potential to do so. The same could be said for the child's ability to reason: he has the potential for logical reasoning, but at this state in life, he is incapable of demonstrating it. Faith, like reason, lies dormant with an infant but needing to be guided so that he or she may mature as a person. Because the family and society are necessary for this guidance, we see that a person is essentially a social being.

Finally, there is also a countercultural quality with infant baptism. Think of Jesus' attitude toward children. For instance, recall the Gospel passage in which a group of parents presents their children to Jesus for his blessing, but the disciples scold them, perhaps considering them an annoyance. Jesus then chides his disciples, "Let the children come to me, do not hinder them; for to such belongs the kingdom of God. Truly, I say to you, whoever does not receive the kingdom of God like a child shall not enter it" (Mk. 10:13–16 RSV). This is no mere sentiment from Jesus. At that time children enjoyed no legal rights; they were the property of their parents. Before the age of seven, a child could be sold into slavery. In contrast, Jesus holds up the children as a model for those who seek the kingdom of God. The child who has nothing receives everything as a gift. So, too, those who wish to follow Christ must open themselves in faith and receive him as a gift. The child becomes a model of faith.

Therefore the church welcomes its members unconditionally, recognizing their divine heritage. Infants are accepted for the promise they hold—the promise of continuing the praise of

God and service to the community. In the hope that one day this promise will bear fruit, the church pledges its support for an infant. For these reasons, the church should baptize babies.

conclusion

At the time of writing this book, the American Atheists Association is planning an advertising campaign. It is the Christmas season, and the association plans to rent billboard space on which will be depicted a traditional setting of the Nativity, showing Joseph and Mary inside a stable leaning over a manger, surrounded by shepherds and farm animals. Underneath the picture a caption reads, "You know it's a myth. This season, believe in reason." As we saw with the proponents of de-baptism, some atheists oppose reason to faith, situating them in separate camps of science (where statements can be proven with certainty) and fantasy (the infantile lair of wish fulfillment).

Now it may strike you as confusing to conclude a study of baptism with such a conflict, citing an argument against initiation into a religious community. But such a conflict can provide a backdrop against which we develop a renewed appreciation for the sacraments and for faith in general. Indeed, this is the culture in which we live, a society influenced by a growing secularism that calls into question the purpose for religion among well-educated and rational citizens.

Unlike the challenge of Communist atheism during the Cold War, which threatened to annihilate Christian faith, modern secularism is willing to tolerate religious faith but wonders skeptically about the purpose it serves, wondering why a reasonable person would choose to believe in something that cannot be proven. However, for the Christian, reason and faith are not sequestered into separate camps. They move together. Pope John Paul II, in his encyclical *Fides et Ratio* ("Faith and Reason"), declares that faith and reason are the two wings needed for flight. Faith guides reason to its proper end, while reason directs faith in its steps along the way. The story of the Nativity is indeed a symbolic story, which evokes meaning as its truth unfolds in the lives of its audience, of those who hear it and live it. We could conclude the Nativity narrative with the words from Jesus' first sermon, delivered in the synagogue at Nazareth: "Today this Scripture is fulfilled in your hearing!" In other words, the story continues enfolding all of humanity in its plot. The believers acknowledge this through baptism, by which they are incorporated into the story of salvation.

In the sacrament of baptism, faith and reason actually converge. Baptism marks the beginning of new life, whether in the physical "newness" of a newborn infant, or the new life which an adult gains from becoming enlightened through the life of faith. Something new happens here that calls for a celebration:

a temporary cessation of the daily order and the expression of gratitude for this new life.

In the case of a newborn infant, reason alone may explain the biological process of her birth and her genetic disposition by which she resembles one or another of her parents. But is it mere fantasy to consider this newborn child a gift, or a symbol of hope? Is it merely wish fulfillment to be moved to express gratitude and to imagine that the heartfelt desire to offer thanks moves one beyond the realm of the temporal toward the transcendent? The same holds true for the adult candidates for baptism: their presence and their personal choice to enter the church provide a symbol of hope for the Christian community, a quiet reassurance that God's work should continue. Their search for God echoes the community's quest, deepening their participation in the story of salvation.

Perhaps the hinge that joins faith and reason in baptism is the recognition of the candidate as a gift. The one who is requesting baptism, or for whom it is requested, is presented to the community in such a way that the community becomes aware of a supreme giver, a generous benefactor concerned with the well-being of humanity. To consider the person as a gift is to recognize that this human being is more than a product of a biological process and that the person's lifelong quest is more than a psychological journey. Rather, this person joins with so many others in the eternal search for the divine. It is a matter of discovering the sacred within the ordinary, of finding the supernatural dwelling amid the natural. And this is not recognized in any sentimental or self-serving way. That is, the divine presence never reveals itself simply to affirm or to amuse but is always accompanied by an invitation to grow in union with God and to realize one's human dignity more fully.

Try to imagine Moses meeting God in the burning bush. In this truly awesome event, Moses is overwhelmed to hear the voice of God and to be invited into the presence of the almighty. In return, Moses is sent to serve the people of God, commissioned as their liberator and lawgiver, a spokesman for the Lord. God calls Moses into union with the divine. This union is a gift. Moses expresses gratitude for the gift through his lifelong service for Israel. In this way, what he received remains with him and Israel throughout their history. In so many ways the Israelites were able to discern the presence of God in nature: in their land, in the events of nature, in their meals, and in one another. For them, the world was indeed charged with the grandeur of God. Much later, a son of Israel, Jesus of Nazareth, waded into the Jordan River and requested to be baptized by John. While John at first refused, confused by the thought of the Messiah bowing before a mortal, John baptized Jesus with river water and once again God's voice was heard, calling humanity into union with its Creator, united through the Son of God. In Christian baptism the faithful venture into the Jordan, joining Jesus, to be washed clean of sin and to hear the Father's pronouncement that we are beloved by God. Like Moses, we slip off our sandals to stand on holy ground and listen to the Lord's commission: we are to lead, liberate, and live in the name of the Lord so that all may attain that same union with God.

Christians rehearse the baptismal story time and again so that we may remember our call—our encounter with the Son of God—and deepen our commitment in gratitude for the gift of faith. The celebration of baptism reminds us that we glean this gift of faith specifically through creation and redemption. Since all created reality manifests the presence of God, we find God's fingerprints throughout all of creation. The newborn and newly converted are able to echo the prophecy spoken by Isaiah (43:19 RSV), "Behold, I am doing a new thing!" We are grateful for the gift of creation and the promise of salvation. In turn we pledge our obedience to God in service to the community into which we are baptized.

Still, human nature is fraught with distraction, making it difficult to keep our pledge. We sometimes fall into ingratitude, forgetting our purpose. But the indelible mark of baptism reminds us that we are never separated from God, and through the sacrament of penance we always return to the font to be washed clean and receive a second chance. The candle of the *illuminadi* offered at the ritual of initiation shines on the path of redemption; we are redeemed, saved from sin. Here too, amid the dross of human sinfulness, God speaks again, "Behold I make all things new!" What some people may have thought was lost, destroyed, or even dead, God returns, restores, and raises to new life. Nothing is damned; rather, everything is sacred.

1 "Doctrine Committee Chairman Gives Rationale for Critiquing *Quest for the Living God*," USCCB, Office of Media Relations, April 18, 2011, http://www.usccb.org/news /archived.cfm?releaseNumber=11-078.

2 St. Augustine of Hippo, *Confessions* 1.1 trans. F. J. Sheed (Indianapolis: Hackett, 1993).

3 *Poems and Prose of Gerard Manley Hopkins*, ed. W. H. Gardner (Middlesex: Penguin Books, 1953), 27. See also Francis X. McAloon, *The Language of Poetry as a Form of Prayer: The Theo-Poetics of Gerard Manley Hopkins* (Lewiston, NY: Edwin Mellen, 2008), 150.

4 Richard McBrien, *Catholicism: Study Edition* (Minneapolis: Winston, 1981), 1180.

5 *Catechism of the Catholic Church* (Liguori, MO: Liguori Publications, 1994), nos. 1996–2005.

6 Paul Tillich, *Dynamics of Faith* (New York: Harper and Row, 1957), 121.

7 *Catechism of the Catholic Church*, no. 1677.

8 While many Protestants do not accept all seven of the Roman Catholic sacraments, these two are generally celebrated. The

reason for this is the "Lord's command," by which he instructs the disciples to continue these practices.

9 See Matt. 10:1–8; Lk. 9:1; 10:1–9.

10 See my chapter "Go in Peace . . . Then What?" in *Living Beauty: The Art of Liturgy*, ed. Alejandro Garcia-Rivera and Thomas Scirghi (Lanham, MD: Rowman and Littlefield, 2008), 143–47.

11 For a contemporary rendering of this classic notion, consider that you have an opportunity to meet the president of the United States. Or, if your political affiliation prohibits such imagining, consider that you will have a private audience with the pope.

12 Aidan Kavanagh, "Christian Initiation in Post-Conciliar Roman Catholicism," in *Living Water, Sealing Spirit: Readings on Christian Initiation*, ed. Maxwell Johnson (Collegeville, MN: Liturgical Press, 1995), 5.

13 An astute observer of the film *Gladiator* may have noticed this seal. Early in the story, the camera focuses briefly on the upper arm of Maximus, the general played by Russell Crowe, and we see the Roman seal "SPQR." A little while later in the story, we see Maximus scraping off this seal from his arm, after having been betrayed by the new emperor, Commodus, the son of Marcus Aurelius, and a fellow officer. The gesture suggests that Maximus is renouncing his affiliation with the Roman army. A man watching Maximus inquires, "Will not your gods grow angry with you?"

14 The word *pagan*, similar to *heathen*, traditionally described a person who is not a Christian, or a Jew, or Muslim. The term derives from the Latin *pagus*, meaning a peasant or a rustic person. Heathen referred to a "heath dweller." In ancient times, this person was associated with the worship of the earth.

15 *Documents of the Baptismal Liturgy*, ed. E. C. Whitaker, revised by Maxwell Johnson (Collegeville, MN: Liturgical Press, 2003), 45.

16 Or consider an example from the first volume of the Harry Potter series, *Harry Potter and the Sorcerer's Stone*. As the story draws to its conclusion, young Harry engages in a fierce fight with his nemesis, the evil Lord Voldemort. Harry is left unconscious, and the reader is not sure if he is alive or dead. But in the next scene, Harry awakes in the infirmary of the Hogwarts School. Standing at his bedside is the school's headmaster, Professor Dumbledore. Harry is surprised to find himself still alive and wonders aloud how he was able to survive the power of Voldemort. The kindly headmaster explains to Harry that his mother, who died to protect him, loved him so much that she left a mark on him. With this mark no evil will overcome him. This mark sealed him, protecting him from the destructive power of evil.

17 "Homily of His Holiness Benedict XVI," Holy Saturday, April 3, 2010, http://www.vatican.va/holy_father/benedict_xvi/homilies/2010/documents/hf_ben-xvi_hom_20100403_veglia-pasquale_en.html, accessed April 4, 2010.

18 Richard McBrien, *Catholicism: Study Edition* (Minneapolis: Winston, 1981), 1240.

19 The word *Pentateuch* refers to the first five books of the Bible: Genesis, Exodus, Leviticus, Numbers, and Deuteronomy. *Pentateuch* is a Greek word meaning "five books." These five books are also called the Torah, which comes from the Hebrew word meaning "law."

20 See 2 Pet. 1:16–19.

21 John McKenzie, "Baptism," *Dictionary of the Bible* (New York: Macmillan, 1979), 79.

22 Karl Barth, *Church Dogmatics* IV/4, *The Doctrine of Reconciliation* (Edinburgh: T & T Clark, 1986), 59.

23 See Roland J. Foley, "Leviticus," in *The New Jerome Biblical Commentary*, ed. Raymond E. Brown, Joseph Fitzmeyer, and Roland Murphy (Englewood Cliffs, NJ: Prentice Hall, 1990), 71–72. Also, Gerard S. Sloyan, *Why Jesus Died* (Minneapolis: Fortress, 1995), 83–87.

24 See Titus 3:5 and 1 Pet. 3:18.

25 Pheme Perkins, "The Gospel According to John," in *The New Jerusalem Bible Commentary* (Englewood Cliffs, NJ: Prentice Hall, 1990), 956.

26 Bruce Metzger and Michael Coogan, *The Oxford Companion to the Bible* (New York: Oxford University Press, 1993), 74.

27 "Christian Initiation: General Introduction," in *The Rites of the Catholic Church* (Collegeville, MN: Liturgical Press, 1990), no. 22.

28 McKenzie, "Baptism," 80.

29 Maxwell Johnson, *The Rites of Christian Initiation: Their Evolution and Interpretation* (Collegeville, MN: Liturgical Press, 1979), 35.

30 *Didache* 7. Cf. Johnson, *Rites*, 35.

31 Johnson, *Rites*, 38.

32 Kenan B. Osborne, OFM, *The Christian Sacraments of Initiation: Baptism, Confirmation, Eucharist* (New York: Paulist Press, 1987), 65.

33 Johnson, *Rites*, 52.

34 John F. Baldovin, SJ, *Bread of Life, Cup of Salvation: Understanding the Mass* (Lanham, MD: Rowman and Littlefield, 2003), 94. See also Ann Riggs, "Word, Sacrament and the Christian Imagination," *Worship* (84, no. 1): 10.

35 Riggs, "Word, Sacrament and the Christian Imagination," 10.

36 Joseph Fitzmeyer, "The Letter to the Galatians," in *The New Jerome Biblical Commentary*, ed. Raymond E. Brown, Joseph Fitzmeyer, and Roland Murphy (Englewood Cliffs, NJ: Prentice Hall, 1990), 789.

37 Ray Noll, *Sacraments: A New Understanding for a New Generation* (Mystic, CT: Twenty-Third Publications, 1999).

38 Angelo Di Beraradino and Basil Studer, eds., *History of Theology I: The Patristic Period*, trans. Matthew J. O'Connell (Collegeville, MN: Liturgical Press, 1996), 361–62.

39 Justin Martyr, *Apology* 61, in Johnson, *Rites*, 38.

40 Johnson, *Rites*, 27.

41 Justin Martyr, *Apology* 65, in Johnson, Rites, 39.

42   Edward Yarnold, "Baptism: Medieval," in *The New Dictionary of Liturgy and Worship*, ed. Paul Bradshaw (Louisville: Westminster John Knox, 2002), 39–41.

43   All three of these sources from the early church are cited from Everett Ferguson's monumental work, *Baptism in the Early Church* (Grand Rapids: Eerdmans, 2009), 362–79, 592–602, 720–23.

44   Yarnold, "Baptism: Medieval," 39–41.

45   *Sacrosanctum Concilium*, n. 62, *Vatican Council II: The Conciliar and Post Conciliar Documents* ed. Austin Flannery, OP (Northport: Costello, 1980), 20.

46   *The Catechism of the Catholic Church*, ed. United States Catholic Conference (Liguori, MO: Liguori Publications, 1994), no. 1212.

47   *The Rites of the Catholic Church*, ed. The International Commission on English in the Liturgy (New York: Pueblo, 1983).

48   Aristotle, *Nicomachean Ethics* 2.1, in *The Basic Works of Aristotle*, ed. Richard McKeon (New York: Random House, 1941).

49   *Rites*, no. 37.

50   The reader should note that this discussion follows from the official instructions published by the church's office on the liturgy. In any particular celebration of baptism, some adaptations may have been made which differ from these instructions. To consult the official instructions see "The Rite of Baptism for Children," in *The Rites of the Catholic Church* (New York: Pueblo, 1990). Families may find it helpful to read these instructions to help plan the baptism of their children.

51   *Rites*, no. 72.

52 "Rite of Funerals," in *The Rites of the Roman Catholic Church* (New York: Pueblo, 1983).

53 According to the instruction, the normal presider for the funeral liturgy is the priest, since he is ordained to serve as the "teacher of faith and minister of consolation" (no. 16). However, the funeral rites, except for the Mass, may be celebrated by a deacon and, for the sake of pastoral necessity, a layperson may celebrate the service (cf. "Rite of Funerals," no. 19).

54 Jerome Murphy O'Connor, "The Second Letter to the Corinthians," in *The New Jerome Biblical Commentary*, ed. Raymond E. Brown, Joseph Fitzmeyer, and Roland Murphy (Englewood Cliffs, NJ: Prentice Hall, 1990), 819.

55 Kerry Hughes, *The Incense Bible* (New York: Haworth, 2007), 21–22.

56 Mary Daly, *Beyond God the Father: Toward a Philosophy of Women's Liberation* (Boston: Beacon Press, 1973), 19.

57 For further discussion of the Trinitarian name of God in baptism, see my *An Examination of the Problems of Inclusive Language in the Trinitarian Formula of Baptism* (Lewiston, NY: Edwin Mellen, 2000).

58 See *A Concise Dictionary of Theology*, ed. Gerald O'Collins, sj, and Edward G. Farrugia, sj (Mahwah, NJ: Paulist Press, 2000), 141.

59 P. J. Hill, "Limbo," in *The New Catholic Encyclopedia* (Washington, DC: The Catholic University of America, 1967), 8:762–65.

60 "The Author of Faith." A papal "bull" is a formal papal document having a *bulla*, or "seal," attached to it.

61 Hill, "Limbo," 8:762–65.

62 International Theological Commission (ITC), "The Hope of Salvation for Infants Who Die Without Being Baptized," approved by Pope Benedict XVI January 19, 2007.

63 ITC, "Hope of Salvation," no. 100.

64 "Funerals for Children," in *The Rites of the Roman Catholic Church* (New York: Pueblo, 1983), no. 82.

65 ITC, "Hope of Salvation," no. 7.

66 "Various Texts for Funerals of Children Who Die before Baptism," in *Rites*, no. 235.

67 *Catholic Household of Blessings and Prayers*, ed. National Conference of Catholic Bishops (Washington, DC: USCC, 1988), 277–78. My emphasis.

68 ITC, "Hope for Salvation," nos. 6, 69.

69 ITC, "Hope for Salvation," no. 66.

70 "Decree on Justification," Council of Trent, sixth session, cited in ITC, "Hope for Salvation," no. 66.

71 ITC, "Hope for Salvation," no. 82.

72 Ibid., no. 101.

73 "De-Baptism at the Texas Freethought Convention," October 26, 2008, http://www.youtube.com/watch?v=Z0Yn6vjktN0, accessed October 28, 2011.

74 I am grateful to my student Gina Carnazzo for researching and compiling the following information in her unpublished paper, "De-Baptism: A Heresy?," May 2009.

75 "Debaptism Ceremony; Act of Apostasy," January 24, 2004, http://www.youtube.com/watch?v=zdn95BIZRNw&feature=rel ated, accessed May 15, 2009.

76 Jim Downey, "De-baptism certificate?," Unscrewing the Inscrutable, March 15, 2009, http://www.unscrewingthe inscrutable .com /blogs/ jim-downey/de-baptism-certificate, accessed October 5, 2010.

77 "Spain's Supreme Court Rules Church Can Keep Baptism Records," Catholic News Service, October 1, 2008, http://www .catholicnews.com/data/stories/cns/0804987.htm, accessed April 9, 2010.

78 National Secular Society, http://www.secularism.org.uk /debaptise-yourself.html, accessed May 16, 2009.

79 William Lee Adams, "De-Baptism Gains a Following in Britain," *Time*, April 14, 2009, http://www.time.com/time /world/article/0,8599,1891230,00.html, accessed May 16, 2009.

80 "100,000 Secular Britons Seek 'De-Baptism,'" Agence France-Presse, March 30, 2009. http://www.google.com/hostednews/afp /article/ALeqM5j XcQ2ho0OglDj7I1WxxVGjFmaZkw

81 Nicole Martinelli, "Debaptism 2.0: Fleeing the Flock Via the Net," June 7, 2007, Wired.com, http://www.wired.com/culture /lifestyle/news/2007/06/debaptism, accessed May 15, 2009.

82 Claudia Gaillard, "Argentine Campaign Urges Catholics to Quit Church," March 4, 2009, http://www.reuters.com/article /lifestyleMolt/idUSTRE5235X420090304, accessed May 16, 2009.

83 The recent *Code of Canon Law* was published in 1983, revising the previous edition of 1917.

84 John P. Beal, *New Commentary on the Code of Canon Law*, ed. John P. Beal, James A. Coriden, and Thomas J. Green (New York: Paulist Press, 2000), 1335–36.

85 Pontifical Council for Legislative Texts, *Actus formalis defectionis ab Ecclesia Catholica*, http://www.vatican.va/roman_curia /pontifical_councils/intrptxt/documents/rc_pc_intrptxt_ doc_20060313_actus-formalis_en.html, accessed October 28, 2011. Hereinafter, *Actus*.

86 *Actus*, no. 2.

87 *Actus*, no. 1.

88 See *Code of Canon Law*, 535 §2; *Actus*, no. 6.

89 *Actus*, no. 7.

90 *The Christian Faith: In the Doctrinal Documents of the Catholic Church*, ed. J. Neuner and J. DuPuis (New York: Alba House, 1996), no. 1414.

91 "Christian Initiation: General Introduction," in *Rites*, nos. 16–17.

92 C. Kiesling, "Infant Baptism," *Worship* (42, no. 10): 617–626, at 617.

On Baptism

Hovda, Robert W. *Celebrating Baptism: A Booklet for Participation in the Baptism of Children*. Washington, DC: The Liturgical Conference, 1970.

Johnson, Maxwell. *The Rites of Christian Initiation: Their Evolution and Interpretation*. Collegeville, MN: Liturgical Press, 2007.

Turner, Paul. *The Hallelujah Highway: A History of the Catechumenate*. Chicago: Liturgy Training Publications, 1994.

Whitaker, E. C., and Maxwell Johnson, eds. *Documents of the Baptismal Liturgy*. Collegeville, MN: Liturgical Press, 2003.

Yarnold, Edward. *The Awe-Inspiring Rites of Initiation: The Origins of the RCIA*. Collegeville, MN: Liturgical Press, 1994.

On Sacraments in General

Bausch, William J. *A New Look at Sacraments*. New London, CT: Twenty-Third Publications, 1999.

Chauvet, Louis-Marie. *The Sacraments: The Word of God at the Mercy of the Body*. Collegeville, MN: Liturgical Press, 2001.

Martos, Joseph. *Doors to the Sacred: A Historical Introduction to Sacraments in the Catholic Church.* Liguori, MO: Liguori/ Triumph, 2001.

Noll, Ray. *Sacraments: A New Understanding for a New Generation.* New London, CT: Twenty-Third Publications, 1999.

Osborne, Kenan B., OFM. *The Chirstian Sacraments of Initiation: Baptism, Confirmation, Eucharist.* Mahwah, NJ: Paulist Press, 1987.

acknowledgments

To those who have inspired, critiqued, and encouraged me along the way, I am grateful. To my colleagues and students of the Theology Department of Fordham University, as well as the staff of Campus Ministry, and to my colleagues and students of the Jesuit School of Theology at Santa Clara University at Berkeley. Each place has provided me with the experience to hone my understanding and appreciation of the sacraments. The parishes of Saint Leo the Great in Oakland, California; Saints Mary and Francis de Sales, now the Cathedral Parish of Christ the Light, also of Oakland; and Saint Mary, Help of Christians, in Aiken, South Carolina: here the Word of God comes alive from the pulpit, at the table, and around the font. The Liturgical Theology Seminar of the North American Academy of Liturgy, who read and discussed the section on "de-baptism" and provided helpful feedback. And finally, my editor, Jon Sweeney, for his careful reading of this manuscript and his patience throughout the project. These friends and colleagues help to reveal the sacred in the ordinary.

About Paraclete Press

Who We Are

Paraclete Press is a publisher of books, recordings, and DVDs on Christian spirituality. Our publishing represents a full expression of Christian belief and practice—from Catholic to Evangelical, from Protestant to Orthodox. We are the publishing arm of the Community of Jesus, an ecumenical monastic community in the Benedictine tradition. As such, we are uniquely positioned in the marketplace without connection to a large corporation and with informal relationships to many branches and denominations of faith.

What We Are Doing

Books

Paraclete publishes books that show the richness and depth of what it means to be Christian. Although Benedictine spirituality is at the heart of all that we do, we publish books that reflect the Christian experience across many cultures, time periods, and houses of worship. We publish books that nourish the vibrant life of the church and its people—books about spiritual practice, formation, history, ideas, and customs.

We have several different series, including the best-selling Paraclete Essentials and Paraclete Giants series of classic texts in contemporary English; A Voice from the Monastery—men and women monastics writing about living a spiritual life today; award-winning literary faith fiction and poetry; and the Active Prayer Series that brings creativity and liveliness to any life of prayer.

Recordings

From Gregorian chant to contemporary American choral works, our music recordings celebrate sacred choral music through the centuries. Paraclete distributes the recordings of the internationally acclaimed choir Gloriæ Dei Cantores, praised for their "rapt and fathomless spiritual intensity" by *American Record Guide,* and the Gloriæ Dei Cantores Schola, which specializes in the study and performance of Gregorian chant. Paraclete is also the exclusive North American distributor of the recordings of the Monastic Choir of St. Peter's Abbey in Solesmes, France, long considered to be a leading authority on Gregorian chant.

Videos

Our videos offer spiritual help, healing, and biblical guidance for life issues: grief and loss, marriage, forgiveness, anger management, facing death, and spiritual formation.

Learn more about us at our website:
www.paracletepress.com, or call us toll-free at 1-800-451-5006.

SCAN
TO
READ
MORE

you may also be interested in ...

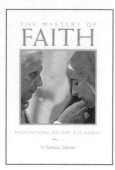

The Mystery of Faith
Meditations on the Eucharist

$17.99 Hardcover | ISBN: 978-1-55725-686-7

Would you like to not just go to Mass, but learn to *live* the Eucharist? Now comes a clear and compassionate voice of encouragement, reflection, and inspiration.

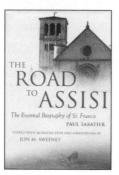

The Road to Assisi
The Essential Biography
of St. Francis

$15.99 Trade paper | ISBN: 978-1-55725-401-6

Discover how the privileged son of a wealthy Italian merchant became the most loved figure in Christian history since Jesus.

Shirt of Flame
A Year with Saint Thérèse of Lisieux

$16.99 Trade paper | ISBN: 978-1-55725-808-3

"What St. Thérèse did for Heather King, she can do for each of us. If you are aching at some very deep places, let this book be your doctor."—RONALD ROLHEISER

Available from most booksellers or through Paraclete Press:
www.paracletepress.com. 1-800-451-5006.